Doing Postgraduate Research

Doing Postgraduate Research

Edited by Stephen Potter

SAGE Publications
London • Thousand Oaks • New Delhi

in association with

SAGE Publications Ltd
6 Bonhill Street
London EC2A 4PU

SAGE Publications Inc.
2455 Teller Road
Thousand Oaks, California 91320

SAGE Publications India Pvt Ltd
32, M-Block Market
Greater Kailash - I
New Delhi 110 048

British Library Cataloguing in Publication data

A catalogue record for this book is available from the British
Library

ISBN 0 7619 4744 2
ISBN 0 7619 4745 0 (pbk)

Library of Congress Control Number available

Text and cover design: barkerhilsdon
Typeset by Photoprint, Torquay, Devon
Printed in Great Britain by The Cromwell Press, Trowbridge,
Wiltshire

Contents

Notes on contributors

Dr. Stephen Potter is a Senior Research Fellow at the Open University. Beginning his career in Social Sciences, he now works in the Technology Faculty's Department of Design and Innovation and is also the Director of the Centre for Technology Strategy. His research and teaching covers design, transport and environmental studies and he is an advisor to government research programmes. Together with David Wield he runs the OU Technology Faculty postgraduate research training programme, and has contributed to a variety of the OU's research training courses and packs.

Dr. Martin Le Voi is a Lecturer in Psychology in the Open University's Social Faculty. His research and teaching centres upon cognitive psychology and the mathematical modelling of memory and cognition. Together with Stephen Potter, he chaired the production of the OU's U500 research training pack and has played a major part in the development of the OU's Master's programme in Social Sciences.

Professor David Wield is the Professor of Innovation and Development in the Open University's Technology Faculty. His teaching centres upon the management of technology and development policies, knowledge and learning in organisations. His recent research has involved studies of technological innovation and East Africa, knowledge management and development. Together with Stephen Potter he runs the OU Technology Faculty postgraduate research training programme, and has contributed to a variety of the OU's research training courses and packs.

Andrew Ward is a consultant to the Open University on study and writing skills.

List of illustrations

Chapter 1

Introduction

Martin Le Voi and Stephen Potter

After reading this chapter you will understand:

- **What sort of book this is**

- **How research really happens**

- **The structure of the book**

A practical generic approach

Welcome to *Doing Postgraduate Research*. This book is intended to help both full and part-time students to do research better, quicker and with as little hassle as possible. *Doing Postgraduate Research* has been developed from an OU training pack (U500, *Doing Academic Research*) that has been used since 1998 by hundreds of part and full-time research students both at the Open University and in other research institutions whose degrees are validated by the Open University. This training material has also been incorporated into a taught OU Master's programme. Not only is the material already widely and successfully used, but it is compliant with UK Research Council training requirements. It formed part of the OU's Mode A research training recognition by the ESRC and has been incorporated into the University's new research training Master's, as required in the 2001 ESRC training guidelines for postgraduate research students.

A key point about the material in *Doing Postgraduate Research* is that it is not a stand-alone book. The authors have not sought to duplicate the various guides that are already available from a number of publishers. The approach of *Doing Postgraduate Research* is different in that we do not believe that any one book can of itself be adequate for any individual's postgraduate training. What we are seeking to do is to provide a flexible core 'study pack', through which we can guide and help you to build materials that are best suited to your own research training needs. This book complements other guides and helps you to sort out how to use a whole range of research training materials. To emphasise the importance of this 'study pack' approach, we regularly refer to two other research training books (see p. 11), and will also refer you to other training sources.

That *Doing Postgraduate Research* is more of a study pack than a book links with the key rationale that what we are seeking to achieve is 'training by doing'. The materials in this book provide research training in conjunction with you doing your own research work; we do not try to teach research skills separately and in abstract. The various chapters include activities that are designed to help you apply what you learn to your project. The training relates to tasks that your supervisor(s) will require you to do anyway (for example, developing a viable research plan and timetable, and doing a review of your topic area).

Another crucial point is that this book contains training materials on generic research processes common to all research students. Sometimes students think that their research can have nothing in common with that conducted by other people in a totally different subject area, and they are sceptical of any attempt at teaching generic aspects. What has an art historian in common with a particle physicist? In fact, for some years now, members of the team that put these materials together have been teaching full-time postgraduates these 'research processes' materials. The students have come from a wide range of topic areas, including laboratory-based scientific experimental work, computer modelling, business, social and educational studies, and philosophy. These students have been very surprised to find how common their experiences are in terms of the sort of processes they have to undertake, and the tips and hints they can exchange.

So *Doing Postgraduate Research* concentrates on tasks that all postgraduate research projects face. These include designing and organising a research project, doing a topic review, writing skills, using computers, considering rights and ethics in research, and the process of the thesis examination and (where held) the oral examination.

Subjects and methods that are specific to your topic or department's area are not included. However, as noted above, a distinctive feature of this book is that it has been designed to guide you when such materials and training should be added. This allows you to develop a customised pack fitting your own needs. The section after next goes into more detail about how the book is organised, and how it can be used together with topic-specific material and training, obtained through either your supervisor(s) or more specific materials and courses (such as Master's courses). If you are doing a research degree, your supervisors are the key link for training in subjects specific to your topic, such as subject-specific literature indices, research methods, data and information sources and analysis methods.

Finally, the book has been designed to be applicable to all types of postgraduate research. The generic research processes covered are therefore of relevance from preparing a taught Master's dissertation through to a PhD, although obviously more depth and detail are required for the latter. Chapter 2 describes what competences each type of degree requires and should guide you in your use of the materials in this book.

How research *really* happens

Before moving on to examine the practicalities of how the book is organised, it is worthwhile thinking a little about the nature of a postgraduate research project, be it a Master's dissertation or a PhD. Quite often textbooks on research suggest that a research project is made up of a series of straightforward tasks, each of which is tackled in sequence. First, there is a review of a topic area from which a research question is selected; then an appropriate research method is chosen, data are gathered and analysed, and the results are written up. In structuring a research report, a thesis or a research article, authors tend to present their research in this sort of logical manner. Although it may be useful for presenting results, in truth research is never as straightforward. Here are two brief accounts by Martin Le Voi of his own PhD research. The first is how it was written up; the second is how it happened.

If you were to read the thesis, this is the way the development of his PhD was presented: it appears to be a linear sequence of development from an early interest in psychology, and specifically memory, through a series of logical experiments to a reasonable conclusion. This linearity of development is, of course, entirely fictional, and, in fact, the research degree developed entirely differently.

BOX 1   My PhD

1   Epistemology

My epistemological position had developed over several years previous to my PhD. I was firmly based in a strongly positivist approach to psychology, committed to controlled experimentation and the development of mathematically based models of human performance.

2   Research area

I was very interested in a new theory of memory developed in Cambridge. It was an elegant mathematical model, which exploited some highly regular empirical results from controlled cued recall experiments, in which cues are given to prompt recall of specific memories.

Also current in the literature was an empirical phenomenon called 'Recognition Failure of Recallable Words'. This was generating some models to account for a highly regular series of results, which I reviewed.

3   Focusing

The published work on Recognition Failure in my view failed to take account of two things: natural forgetting rates in memory and sophisticated 'Signal Detection' models of recognition. My research design developed an experimental series based on these.

4   Data collection and analysis

I ran two experiments collecting data on cued recall and recognition. The data behaved in a very orderly manner, and I was able to develop an original and very simple mathematical model of the forgetting phenomena.

5   Other extensions to the methodology

I extended the cued recall procedure to examine other temporally based phenomena in human memory based around interference, and again showed orderly behaviour in a series of experiments.

6   Overall results

I brought the results together by showing how these experiments related to each other and the current literature, and the possible impact of these models of cued recall on future research.

BOX 2   Life as a research student

Having written a proposal based on looking at some aspects of cued recall, by the time I started my PhD some very new results on subliminal perception (which involves asking participants to respond to stimuli displayed so fast they think they have not seen anything at all) were very interesting, so I started to set up some pilot experiments on these using photographed stimuli and automatic pictorial displays. However, I had some data collected over the summer on skills and handedness, so I also started to write up this work. I decided to do it on a computer, which in those days (1975) was a large IBM 360 central computer whose only input device was a card reader. So to begin with I was simultaneously:

1 Reading about subliminal perception.
2 Learning how to use a card punch machine (a large beast weighing about a ton), and using software called 'Dormat' for creating reports (I would hesitate to glorify this software with the epithet 'word processor').
3 Producing materials for an experiment in psychology.
4 Attending the two departmental seminar series on psychological research.
5 Attending computing courses to learn to program computers (in Fortran).

Eventually I managed to run the experiments and data analysis was added to these activities. This entailed using statistical programs on the IBM so, again, substantial training was involved. A second experiment was planned and production of materials initiated. About this time the central computer introduced a spanking new input device called a Cathode Ray Terminal (CRT) and, using software improbably called GUTS (Gothenburg University Terminal System), data could be input to the computer without walking around with armfuls of punched cards. Somehow it still seemed to generate vast amounts of paper and everything had to be done with card 'images'. I was still using the infamous Dormat software for 'word processing'. However, GUTS was to be the way my thesis was written up, so time spent learning it paid off. GUTS was an incredible advance: a colleague finishing two years before me kept his PhD in six large boxes of punched cards.

　　Simultaneously I began learning to use a new-fangled mini-computer called a PDP-11 in the department: very soon this experience was going to pay off. It used a teletype for input and output. The memory in this computer amounted to 16 Kb (my current PC has 16 Mb).

　　After the second experiment I had a mass of data and spent a few months analysing it. I used most of the statistical methods you can think of – analysis of variance, cluster analysis, even automatic interaction detectors – but eventually I had to conclude I was analysing a set of random numbers! Two years later I found several other researchers had failed to get meaningful results out of subliminal perception experiments.

At this point (half-way through year 2) I decided to throw away all this empirical work and start again, looking at models of recognition failure. Of course, I had been reading about it at the same time anyway.

Although I discarded two experiments, my first year had not been wasted. Nowadays it would be easily recognised as being substantially involved in research training. I had learned lots of computing, including the data analysis packages I needed, and the 'word processing' package I would use to write up. I had written a research report. I had practised running experiments. I had given presentations in departmental research seminars. I had got to know the leading-edge technology for computer-controlled experimentation in the shape of the PDP-11. This knowledge all paid off. Once I made the switch to the memory experiments, it was possible to design, set up and run an experiment in only two weeks. The later experiments were designed to analyse themselves automatically. A year later I had plenty of experimental data for a PhD, and gave up my studentship six months early for a good job at the Open University. Writing up was slowed significantly by shoehorning it in with employment, but it all worked out in the end.

The point of this example is to show how doing research is not a linear process. You will always be doing several things at the same time, which will all impinge upon each other. For example, although you will do a literature review to focus on your research topic, you will also draw on what other researchers have done to help plan your project, the method used, how data are gathered and analysed, how reports are written, and to relate your own findings and conclusions to the existing body of research. It is a continuous interaction – not a self-contained stage from which you move on. Most other research 'stages' similarly have feedback links. Postgraduate, and all academic research, may be better thought of as a flow diagram, around which you will go several times between key boxes, until you exit at the bottom (at least for the purpose of your degree). Figure 1.1 is a diagrammatic representation, labelled with the titles of the chapters of this book (and with subject-specific processes for completeness in unshaded boxes).

Note also how Martin developed his skills through the first eighteen months of his studentship and how he came to look upon the topic in a totally different way. A danger point was when he 'decided to throw away all this empirical work and start again'. Most research degrees have a low point like this. But Martin had learned so much about organising and doing research that he could rapidly adapt his plans. Planning your research, reviewing your plans, and coping with change and problems are all part of the research process, and they are all important themes in this book. Your research will *not* go smoothly!

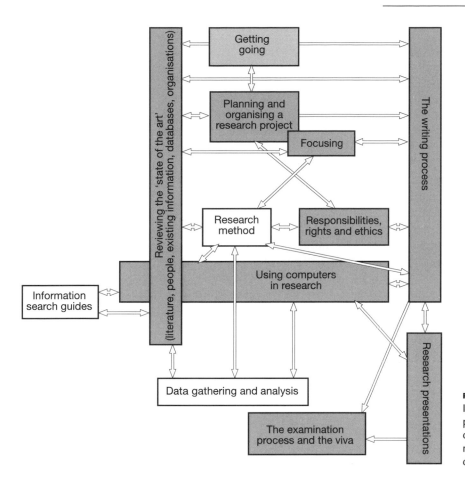

FIGURE 1.1
Interacting
processes in
doing a
research
degree

Organisation of *Doing Postgraduate Research*

We must re-emphasise that *Doing Postgraduate Research* is designed to be used in conjunction with your supervisor(s) or in the context of a Master's course. It in no way replaces the role of research students' supervisors, but it has been designed to support their role in supporting you. We hope that supervisors will use the materials in this book to set you exercises to develop your skills as you progress through your research project. The exercises have been designed so that they can be used by supervisors and can also be used in workshop sessions.

Your supervisor(s), or others in your department, should also advise you of subject-specific training, books, CD-ROMs and advice to be used in conjunction with Doing Postgraduate Research. As was mentioned above, this is how the book has been designed to be used. If you are studying a Master's course, these functions will be provided by your other course materials.

The structure of *Doing Postgraduate Research*

We have organised *Doing Postgraduate Research* to reflect the fact that research requires you to do several things at once, and involves an 'iterative' process of feedback loops. Each activity affects and is affected by another. Consequently the chapters of this book are not intended to form a simple linear sequence; rather, you should go to each chapter for insight and advice as the need arises. Nevertheless, we had to establish a starting-off point (Chapter 2, rather obviously entitled 'Getting going'). Some chapters are of most relevance early on in your research project (for example, 'Planning and organising a research project'), while others mainly fit in later (particularly 'The examination process and the viva'). But even these contain material and issues of relevance throughout your research. For example, Chapter 2, 'Getting going', describes the competences you have to demonstrate in your research degree; Chapter 8, 'The examination process and the viva', notes things that you should plan early. For example, you should build up experience of answering questions on your research, so this chapter should not be left unread until after you have handed in your thesis.

The chapters of *Doing Postgraduate Research* are summarised below, together with an estimate of the amount of time it may take to study them. The timings refer to roughly how long it will take to go through the material and associated activities. Of course, in practice you are unlikely to simply work your way through an individual chapter but, rather, will draw upon it as needed.

1   *Introduction*. Here you are! This chapter is broadly intended to give you an understanding of how to use the book and how it is organised.

2   *Getting going*. This chapter acts as a starting-off point for Doing Postgraduate Research and has two major aims:

1   To work through what you want to achieve in your research degree or Master's dissertation.
2   To help you develop the first steps involved in starting a research project.

More specifically this will involve:

1   Finding out the standards expected.
2   Exploring what are realistic expectations of your degree.
3   Relating your research to your motivations for taking a research degree.
4   Working through the initial steps of doing your research.
5   Exploring the nature of the support provided by your supervisor(s).
6   Identifying other support services provided by your University.

STUDY TIME

It should take about twelve hours to complete all of this chapter.

3 *Planning and organising a research project.* This chapter takes you through how to plan and organise your project. After you have completed it, you should be able to do the following:

1   Produce a preliminary work plan for discussion with your supervisor(s), which will:

      (a) Clarify the focus of your research project.
      (b) Describe the activities needed, and prioritise the order in which they may be accomplished.
      (c) Identify milestones that are achievable.

2   Estimate the amount of time that can reasonably be spent on your project and plan the use of that time, in detail, over the first year.
3   Give a twenty-minute presentation on your chosen research topic and preliminary plan of action.
4   Gain in confidence that a wide range of research tasks are achievable during the first year.

STUDY TIME

This is a substantial and important part of the book and you should allow eighteen to twenty hours to complete it.

4 *The writing process.* Writing is obviously a vital part of doing a research degree or Master's dissertation and it is important that you should get into the habit of writing as soon as you start. There is more to writing than just using the correct academic style; writing a research thesis is a major undertaking, which can easily result in grief. Professional writers have several tricks to help them write to deadlines and to overcome 'writer's block'. This chapter advises you how to approach writing consistently and professionally. You cannot develop good writing habits too early!

STUDY TIME

About twelve hours.

5 *Undertaking a topic review.* A 'topic' or 'literature' review of the state of the art in your study area is a crucial part of any research project. The main focus of this chapter is on planning your information search and the research purposes of doing such a review in your subject area. The term 'topic review' is used to emphasise that more than literature is involved in doing a review, covering electronic information sources and people as informants as well as written sources. There are a number of guides (both on paper and on-line) to the techniques of information searching for several topic areas, including one provided on-line by the Open University Library. We assume that you will obtain one of these to use in conjunction with this section. In particular, this chapter aims to assist you to:

1 Establish the purposes for which you are doing a topic review.
2 Plan and organise your topic review.
3 Identify sources of information.
4 Document your topic review.
5 Write up your topic review.

STUDY TIME

Depending on your experience of literature or information searching, you should allow ten to twelve hours for this chapter, although obviously doing the searches for your review is in addition to this.

6 *Using computers in research.* Nowadays, computers are an essential component of nearly all research. As well as direct use for such purposes as data analysis, electronic bibliographic searches and thesis writing, they have an indirect use because of the Internet, which has transformed communication for many academics and can provide you with an enormous amount of information.

This chapter introduces the possible uses of computers for your work, and indicates some of the software packages you may need. It does not give assistance in using specific software packages, but it does indicate where to find help and training on the ones relevant to you. The topics covered are:

1 Writing a thesis with a word processor.
2 Spreadsheets.
3 Presentation graphics and drawing.
4 Databases.
5 Integrated packages.
6 Project management.
7 Communications.
8 The World Wide Web.
9 Information search.
10 Specialist analytical software.

STUDY TIME

About four to six hours.

7 *Responsibilities, rights and ethics.* Doing research is often a public act (PhD theses end up in the university's library for public use), and with that come responsibilities. This chapter introduces those responsibilities and the rights people have over their intellectual property. Some research can be intrusive or potentially harmful to other living beings or the environment. If your work involves this, you need to be aware of the ethical issues. This chapter provides the ethical guidelines of professional organisations that may be relevant to your work. The topics covered are:

1 Responsibilities.
2 Academic integrity.
3 Accuracy and honesty.
4 Plagiarism.

5 Confidentiality.
6 Using computers.
7 The Data Protection Act.
8 Health and Safety.
9 Intellectual property rights and copyright.
10 Ethics.

STUDY TIME

About eight to ten hours.

8 *The examination process and the viva.* This chapter is intended to assist you to:

1 Explore the purposes of a viva.
2 Understand how your examiners are appointed.
3 Understand what your examiners are required to do.
4 Prepare for your viva.

STUDY TIME

About six hours.

Set books and other support materials

As already mentioned, the approach of this book is that it constitutes a study pack around which you will build further research training materials. As such we purposely do not make it self-contained and, in particular, we draw upon two 'set books' that complement the materials provided. These two moderately priced books are:

Estelle M. Phillips and D. S. Pugh, *How to Get a PhD*, third edition (2000), Open University Press, Buckingham.
Pat Cryer, *The Research Student's Guide to Success*, second edition (2000), Open University Press, Buckingham.

How to Get a PhD is written by two experienced academics about the process of getting a PhD. Despite the title, most of the content is relevant to students doing other research degrees as well. Having studied the actual experience of research students, the authors cover aspects of a research programme that you may not have considered before, such as ways of gaining control of your supervision sessions. The book gives some good advice on how to proceed in many difficult areas.

The Research Student's Guide to Success is also written by an experienced academic who has studied research students' progress. It is designed for students doing a range of research degrees and postgraduate dissertations. Like *Doing Postgraduate Research*, the book concentrates on the key generic processes and tasks involved in research and is sensitive to the diversity of approaches to research from both students and supervisors.

The set books are used throughout *Doing Postgraduate Research* but they also contain general advice on doing research. Some helpful offprints are also included in this book, which you should read in conjunction with the relevant chapter. Do ask your supervisor to recommend any research guides and methods books that are particularly appropriate to your topic area, or look for recommended reading in your Master's course material.

Other support materials are suggested in the individual chapters. There are a number of study skill guides available that would complement this book. Sage Publications have a Study Skills range which includes:

P. Redman, *Good Essay Writing* (2001), Sage Publications, London.
N. Walliman, *Your Research Project* (2000), Sage Publications, London.
K. Rudestam and R. Newton, *Surviving Your Dissertation* (2000), Sage Publications, London.

The Open University also produces a range of *Good Study Guides* to help students, both beginners and experienced alike, to develop successful study techniques. Each one includes key study skills such as effective reading and note-taking, writing skills, working with numbers, and preparing for examinations. In addition, there are exercises, examples and specific study advice relevant to their subject areas. Four titles are currently available (the first is generic, the other three cover specific study areas):

A. Northedge, *The Good Study Guide* (1990), Open University Press, Buckingham.
A. Northedge *et al.*, *The Sciences Good Study Guide* (1997), Open University Press, Buckingham.
E. Chambers, *The Arts Good Study Guide* (1997), Open University Press, Buckingham.
E. Giles and N. Hedge, *The Manager's Good Study Guide* (1994), Open University Press, Buckingham.

The OU version of this research training material (the U500 *Doing Academic Research* pack) has a page within the OU Library's open access site. It provides useful internet Web links that contain further information and support the section of this book's training material. It is to be found at: http://routes.open.ac.uk/ROUTES/subject-listing/Courses/U500.html Alternatively go to the OU home page at http://www.open.ac.uk and go from there to the library site, within which (under Quick Links) is the Routes home page (http://routes.open.ac.uk/) containing the U500 entry.

And finally ...

Your schooldays are said to be the best years of your life. But nothing can quite match doing your own research. If you are lucky enough to be studying for a research degree, it is a time when you can do research relatively free of the hassle of writing interim reports for research councils, when you can pursue a research programme with a singlemindedness and dedication to purpose few can achieve after finishing. So enjoy it, *relish* it, and you can be sure of a unique and sometimes exhilarating experience!

Chapter 2

Getting Going

Stephen Potter

After reading this chapter you will be able to:

- Relate your research to your motivations for taking a research degree

- Explore what are realistic expectations of your research degree

- Find out the standards expected of your research degree

- Work through the initial steps of undertaking your research degree

- Explore the nature of the support provided by your supervisors

- Identify other support services provided by the university

This chapter is intended to help you to:

1   Identify what you want to achieve in your research degree or dissertation.
2   Develop the first steps involved in starting a research project.

Other chapters will develop these initial steps in more detail, particularly Chapter 3, 'Planning and organising a research project'. However, it is worthwhile getting a strategic overview first. Material in several chapters of Cryer (2000) will be used and this chapter also draws on Phillips and Pugh (2000).

A number of activities are suggested in this chapter. One idea suggested in this book is to keep a 'research journal' in which you note ideas and thoughts on the development of your project. (This idea is detailed in the first section of Chapter 3.) It would be useful to keep the notes on these activities in your research journal.

This chapter obviously deals with the initial stages of a research project but you will probably need to refer to it frequently as your research progresses. For example, the section on demonstrating what is expected of a research degree is of relevance to writing your thesis and preparing for your viva.

Why am I doing this?

> **ACTIVITY 2.1**
>
> First, simply jot down why you want to do a research degree (or dissertation topic). Try to be as specific as possible.
> Also note down what, when you have finished, you expect to come out of your work in terms of:
>
> 1 Results.
> 2 You personally.
> 3 What you will be able to do that you could not do before.
>
> **READING**
> After you have done this activity, read the section 'Aims of students' on student motivations in chapter 3 of Phillips and Pugh (pp. 24–6 of the third edition) and the first part of chapter 4 (the section 'Not wanting a PhD', pp. 33–5). Make notes on any points that strike a chord in your life. Then move on to read the first part of chapter 2 in Pat Cryer's book, which explores reasons for undertaking a research degree. (In the second edition this is from p. 12 up to the activity on p. 14.) There could be additions to Pat Cryer's list of reasons. For a start, 'failing to follow a girlfriend to Finland' could be added from Phillips and Pugh.

When supervising and training both Master's and PhD students, I have come across strong ethical and personal reasons for people wishing to do a research degree, varying from environmental concern to trying to sort out why parents are so frustratingly indifferent to school governing structures seeking their involvement. I suppose these could go under the category of 'contributing to knowledge', but I do not think the people involved saw it that way.

The following quotation is from an OU research degree student, Piers Worth, who undertook a PhD in the Institute for Educational Technology, looking at the relationship between creativity and age. This is a subject that spans cognitive psychology and adult development. Piers started as a part-time student and then moved on to full-time study.

> I had a very demanding full-time job, and was struggling as a part-time OU student. Generally I do what I do well – and yet I knew that was becoming increasingly likely to be untrue if I kept on the way I was as a part-time student. Jane Henry [his internal supervisor] helped incredibly by setting me a very specific schedule, and I was responding, yet I think that danger of failure was still there.
>
> So I was facing the question what to do. I knew I loved what I was studying. Passionate about it is not too strong a word. I knew I didn't want to get 'old' and find I had not done this – I knew I could not not do the study. So that prompted me into asking and asking about applying for a full-time place. And when I took the decision to try, so many things just seemed to fall into place to help me do it.
>
> Undoubtedly I was doing a PhD with future work/career in mind. Yet as I have moved through I am staggered by what I am learning about me, and finding me changing as a result. I think this may be made 'easier' or more likely in that I am working with people on biographies and their own work processes, so I am prompted into looking at myself as this unfolds.

Note how Piers has found his motivations deepen and develop through his PhD. In commenting on a draft of this text, a member of our academic staff reflected on what motivated her to undertake a PhD:

> In my own case, career progression was probably a key driver. I was working in an administrative job (in the NHS) but wanted to become more involved in policy making or consultancy. Experience in job applications suggested that 'an administrator' was not regarded as having the right skills for such work! Doing a PhD enabled me to become more expert both in terms of subject matter and transferable research skills. It also enabled me to use concepts and theories I had become interested in through OU undergraduate studies which were more difficult to apply in my everyday work. (As it turned out I ended up staying at the OU but that's another story!)

Cryer's distinction between 'essential' reasons for undertaking a research degree and 'supporting' reasons is a good way to think about motivations.

ACTIVITY 2.2

List what you consider to be 'essential' and 'supporting' reasons for under-taking a research degree or dissertation topic. Use Cryer's listing, the Phillips and Pugh examples, my comments above and any experiences and thoughts of your own to make up the list.

Essential reasons might include:

1   Personal development.
2   To be able to make a difference – for example, a desire to change practice at work or to learn more about a 'condition' that students or members of their family have experienced.
3   Burning interest in a topic (intellectual curiosity).
4   Career progression.
5   To keep one's mind active.

For example, one external student I supervised, when he retired, undertook a PhD to apply some work he had done in his job (the development of fuel cells) to a topic that deeply interested him – pollution from road traffic. A student doing an MA at Brunel University recognised that he was not cut out for teaching schoolchildren and sought a career change to become a design manager in industry. Following a work placement associated with his MA, he secured a very satisfying job with that company.

Another research student developed a strong interest in Roman social history during her first degree. She was unable to follow this up at the time but, finding herself at home with small children, felt she had to do something to keep her mind active and registered for a BPhil. Another student undertook a very specific PhD study into the properties of new composite materials specifically with the aim of pursuing an industrial career in a closely related job.

Supporting reasons might include:

1   Current job is a dead end.
2   For the experience.
3   Employer sponsorship is available.

Personal circumstances can play an important part and constrain your choices. A mature student with a family may purposely constrain their choice of where to study. I know full well that personal circumstances affected my decision to accept a studentship at the OU, in that my girlfriend and I had just got engaged. Sorting out whether, after we were married, living in Milton Keynes was compatible with her commuting to London was a pretty important thing to take into account. Nonetheless, just because the studentship fitted well with our developing relationship was not in itself an essential reason to do the PhD topic that I chose. I suspect situations like ours arise pretty often.

Remember, Cryer notes that many research students who register for the 'wrong' reasons end up being motivated by 'right' reasons. Phillips and Pugh paint a somewhat more negative picture of the dangers of starting a PhD for the wrong reasons. It is very hard to complete a research degree (a PhD in particular) just because the grant is there and a project exists. Your personal motivation is crucial.

As I noted in my own case, the boundary between 'wrong' and 'right' reasons may be blurred. For example, the career/job aspect can fall between categories. Perhaps the difference is whether someone is simply trying to escape from one job or is positively running towards another. My wife, for example, was stuck with a dead-end job until an MA at the Royal College of Art provided her with the opportunity to shift to a new career that really excited her (and still does). She was looking not for something to help her run away but for something to run to. The example above of the MA student who wanted to leave teaching also falls into this category, as he had a clear idea of where he wanted to go.

ACTIVITY 2.3

Return to what you wrote down in Activity 2.1. How do your own reasons relate to your categories of essential and supporting reasons for doing a research degree?

Discussion

Cryer does a similar activity in her book and says that research students need to have, at least in part, motives that are intellectual. I would add that it is perfectly acceptable to have a core motivation that is not intellectual but can be fulfilled in an intellectual way. For example, an environmental campaigner may find a research degree a good way to work through strongly held ethical beliefs. Others do this by organising campaigns or political action, but researching a key issue and publicising the results is a perfectly valid way of working through such a motivation.

This raises the question of whether a research degree is the right way to work through your motivations. In some cases I have advised students against registering for a research degree because it would not satisfy their core motivations. In one case, an external student realised this after being registered for a year for a PhD, and instead did a full-time vocational taught Master's, which suited his needs much better.

Overall, do not be apologetic about what motivates you to undertake your research. Even if you need to be a little more realistic about what you can achieve (more on that below), your motivations are still what started you out on this work – and what will keep you going. You are bound to have days (possibly weeks) when things are really tough. When this happens, perhaps turning back to your notes on the first activity of this chapter may help.

Research degree requirements

What is achievable in a research degree

Having thought about motivations for undertaking a research degree, it is worthwhile noting that, even if you are doing your research for the 'best' intellectual reasons, you need to have a clear idea of what can or cannot be achieved in a research degree. Most of the rest of this chapter is intended to help you to explore this question.

First, it is important to note that this section assumes the British concept of a PhD degree. Although the British concept of a PhD is shared by the education systems of many other countries, it is important to emphasise that concepts of what constitutes a PhD do vary. In some places (for example, Germany and some other northern European countries) the education system is different and PhDs are seen as proof by experts in a field of their leading position. As a result, these sorts of PhD take much longer to complete than in the United Kingdom. In the United States, PhDs can also take longer than in the United Kingdom, but there is less standardisation. In general, US PhDs involve a long route through taught postgraduate classes, together with a written thesis. However, in some US universities it can be acceptable for the thesis to be an applied research project with no theoretical or conceptual contribution. Such a research project would be considered unacceptable in the United Kingdom. Pages 214–15 of Phillips and Pugh (2000) contain more details about the US-style PhD.

Quite apart from these differing concepts of a PhD, students do have a tendency to be overambitious. This is a crucial problem in the early stages of virtually all research projects. Even a PhD cannot accommodate a life's work. If you think that your research project is going to result in you producing the ultimate in your topic area, or shift the whole way in which your subject is studied (a so-called 'paradigm shift'), you will have real problems. Even the continental concept of a PhD does not go that far!

Many students start off by viewing a PhD (and other research degrees) in this way ('My life's work'). It is an unrealistic expectation. Phillips and Pugh point out that Einstein's theory of relativity was:

> not [his] PhD thesis (that was a sensible contribution to Brownian motion theory). *Das Kapital* was not Marx's PhD (that was on the theories of two little-known Greek philosophers). Of course, while doing their PhDs Einstein and Marx were undoubtedly preparing themselves for the great questionings that led to the big shifts, but they were also demonstrating their fully professional mastery of the established paradigms.
>
> (Phillips and Pugh, 2000, p. 36)

Although your research degree will show that you know what you are doing in your topic area, it is not a requirement that you must prove yourself to be the best in the world. Your research degree can be part of your own lifelong learning, but it will be something from which you will continue to learn and grow. On the other hand, your research degree should be able to produce something that is useful and fulfilling in terms of your core motivations. You can add a few pieces to a jigsaw that were not there before.

Doing too little is also a problem, but this is usually a misunderstanding about the academic nature of a research degree. This issue is explored further in the next section, but it is worth considering here, if only to juxtapose it with the 'life's work' misconception of a research degree.

Phillips and Pugh (2000, pp. 38–9) highlight the danger of underestimating or not understanding the sort of research that is required. This can be a real danger for part-time students who work, for example, in journalism, marketing or some types of applied industrial research. Their experience in these areas, although very valuable, can lead to a research approach that is inadequately rigorous for an academic qualification. This can also be true of people from a campaigning/pressure group background. While representing valuable experience, the methods of gathering and using evidence in such a 'political' context may not be appropriate to a research degree.

One academic had a salutary experience as an external examiner for a PhD in another university where the student, from overseas, seemed to have been sent to the United Kingdom to do a PhD that would solve a problem that his government had about installing new computer systems. Unfortunately the resulting thesis was theory-free and descriptive (and hence not a PhD – or at least not yet). The student would have been better off with an MSc in computer science with a relevant dissertation.

Phillips and Pugh emphasise that all research degrees are about training in your area, and that this should show you are a competent researcher. If you think of your research degree as essentially a training qualification you are likely to hit the right standard for a UK research degree.

ACTIVITY 2.4

If you have any concerns emerging from what you have done and read in this section, make sure you discuss them with your supervisor.

What is expected of a research degree

This part looks at what is expected of a research degree and a dissertation that is part of a taught Master's degree. Although all these involve undertaking a research project, what you have to demonstrate in your research, and the competences required, differ. It is therefore useful to have an overview of what competences you need to show for each type of degree. This should help you to pitch your research at the right level for the degree you are taking.

This section uses as its basis the Open University's regulations and definitions for its research degrees, although reference will be made to the guidance and regulations from other UK universities. The research degree regulations of all UK universities are required to meet nationally agreed standards; thus it is appropriate to structure this section around the OU regulations. However, the types of research degree offered and the details of the regulations do vary between UK universities. If you are registered with another university, you must check up on the wording used in your regulations and discuss with your supervisor(s) any important differences from those detailed below.[1]

The Open University offers three research degrees, BPhil, MPhil and PhD. A number of universities offer only MPhil and PhD qualifications, and it seems likely that the BPhil (Bachelor of Philosophy) degree may soon cease to exist as universities implement the two-level QAA Qualifications Framework.

It is useful to look at the OU award regulations to see what is required of the university's three degrees. In the written report they make after reading a thesis and undertaking a viva the examiners are required to state how the student has (or has not) fulfilled these requirements. (see Chapter 8 on the examination and viva.)

Bachelor of Philosophy (BPhil). This involves a research programme or a literature review of a given field that must show evidence of:

1   Ability to investigate critically a specific field of study.
2   Adequate knowledge and discussion of the literature of that field.
3   Good style and presentation.
4   A significant advance in your field beyond first-degree level.

(Maximum 60,000 words.)

Master of Philosophy (MPhil). This involves a research programme that must show evidence of:

1   Proficiency in the methods and techniques of research.
2   Good style and presentation.
3   Adequate knowledge and discussion of the literature in your specific field of study.
4   Initiative and independence of thought.
5   A distinct contribution to scholarship.

(Maximum 60,000 words.)

A dissertation as part of a taught Master's course is at this level. The Master's will have taught these competences and the dissertation is intended to show that the student is able to apply them. The dissertation is, of course, much shorter than an entire Master's degree by research. This will be set by the course, but it is typically under 20,000 words.

Doctor of Philosophy (PhD). This involves a research programme that must show evidence of:

1   Good presentation and style.

2   A significant contribution to knowledge.
3   The capacity to pursue further research without supervision.
4   A significant amount of material worthy of publication.

(Maximum 100,000 words.)

You should note that one thing that does vary between institutions is the specified maximum length of a thesis. For example, De Montfort University's regulations specify the following as the 'normal' maximum number of words:

In Science and Engineering and Art and Design, for PhD	40,000
In Science and Engineering and Art and Design, for MPhil	20,000
In Arts, Social Sciences and Education, for PhD	80,000
In Arts, Social Sciences and Education, for MPhil	40,000

However, this limit does exclude 'ancillary data' that would appear in an appendix.

There is a specified range where the presentation or submission consists substantially of material in other than written form, which is:

For PhD   10,000–12,000 words
For MPhil   6,000–8,000 words

Sometimes the maximum length is specified in terms of pages rather than words. A 250 page limit is one example that I have come across.

When considering a maximum word limit or number of pages you should realise that it is not a target to aim for! Word limits exist for several reasons. They are for the examiners' benefit, in that it would be unreasonable to require an examiner to wade through a 300,000 word text. However, given that, in your research degree, you are proving your ability as a researcher, the central rationale is that you should be able to produce a reasonable-size research report on your project. An overlength thesis or dissertation would suggest that a student still has much to learn about organising and writing a research report.

The OU word limits allow for research methodologies that require a lot of written information to be reported (for example, discourse analysis or where detailed case studies are involved), and so most research degrees should be well below the maximum limits. This particularly applies to scientific research degrees, which can be considerably shorter than those in the humanities. The regulations of De Montfort University reflect this difference between disciplines, and their guidelines where non-written presentations are involved show by how much a thesis may be shortened. The OU regulations take a different approach in that they specify a higher, but generic, word limit.

ACTIVITY 2.5

Note down the key differences between the competences that need to be shown for each type of degree. Competences are the sorts of knowledge, skill and understanding required rather than particular tasks. The next section explores this issue.

Competences required for a research degree

It is worthwhile working through the competences required for the Bachelor, Master's and doctorate research degrees. As well as the PhD student attempting to take on too much (the 'last word in … /life's work' view of a PhD), there is also a danger of those undertaking an MPhil trying to do a PhD project. Activity 2.5 asked you to note down the difference in the competences needed for these three levels. As you should have noticed, besides the universal requirement of 'good style and presentation', the requirements are cumulative: a higher-level degree will also require a demonstration of the skills and competences of the degree below it. So I will start by looking at what is expected of a BPhil and then move on to what in addition is required of the Master's and doctorate levels.

Competences required for all research degrees

Good presentation and style are expected of all research degree theses and dissertations. Sometimes the regulations of a university imply rather than explicitly state the need for good presentation and style. However, writing well and coherently is a fundamental competence needed for any research degree. Academic writing is covered in Chapter 4. However, activity 2.6 can be useful in terms of thinking about how the writings of others succeed (or not) in getting their message across.

ACTIVITY 2.6

In reviewing the literature, instead of considering the articles or books that represent the 'leading edge' of your subject in content and method, look at them in terms of presentation. How well do they communicate the research to you? Pick out two or three that you feel are the best at doing this and two or three you feel are bad. Make a list of what makes the good ones good and the bad ones bad. (This activity can be combined with your work on 'Familiarising yourself with research standards', p. 28).

Critically reviewing existing research and knowledge in your subject area is a part of all research degrees. A BPhil most commonly involves writing a review of a particular subject area. For a Master's or a doctorate such a review is then expected to be a springboard for further original work. The MPhil and PhD research degree regulations for De Montfort University develop this requirement a little further, specifying 'a critical investigation and evaluation of the topic of research'. All other university regulations contain some similar phrase.

Chapter 5 deals in detail with undertaking a 'state of the art' topic review and how it links into other research tasks, so it will not be discussed here. However, at this point it is worthwhile looking at what such a review should achieve, i.e. it must demonstrate:

1   Your ability to investigate critically a specific field of study (i.e. to evaluate what has been done).
2   An adequate knowledge and discussion of the literature of that field.

If these two criteria are met, you will more or less automatically fulfil the other main criterion for a BPhil of showing that you have made *a significant advance in your field beyond first-degree level*. (This is obviously necessary for all other research degrees as well.)

The key phrase in this first criterion is the term 'investigate critically'. It is not just about producing a list of what others have done in your topic area; it is about demonstrating that you understand it, showing, for example, if you can say whether a particular contribution makes sense, fits in or disagrees with what others have said, and is important or not. The wording of the De Montfort regulations, using the word 'evaluation', puts emphasis on demonstrating your critical abilities.

This links into the second criterion of *an adequate knowledge and discussion of the literature*. 'Adequate knowledge' does not mean following up every minor piece of work, but making sure that you cover the major writers and their work. This is very much about discernment – that you do not miss out anything important, but equally that you do not become sidetracked by following up every triviality. Adequate knowledge also includes the ability to discern where the literature is thin, or where there are gaps in knowledge.

At the Master's level, research will be more specialist than for a BPhil (and even more so will that for a PhD). In consequence, you need to show that you can identify the boundaries of your specific area, and can draw out from the wider literature lessons that are of importance to your more tightly defined topic. Take the analogy of an explorer writing a guidebook about a new country they have discovered, which is to be used by others who are planning to visit. The guidebook would have to identify the major places worth visiting, how to get to them, how important they were and how they related to each other. A series of unrelated photographs with simple captions is no guidebook.

An example of how these criteria can be fulfilled arose when planning a BPhil study with one of my external research students. The subject area was local authority integrated transport strategies and how they address the issue of environmental sustainability. Central to this would be a review of the published transport strategies of local authorities, plus academic and other literature on this subject. In order to provide a structure and focus, the student would first explore definitions of integration, with respect to transport planning, and what is considered to be environmentally sustainable in transport. This would allow the development of a typology into which the local authority strategies could be placed, according to the definitions used and associated actions proposed. This typology would form the structure for the critique of local transport strategies, and would show which ones represent 'best practice' and whether they are adequate for the environmental challenges identified. It is this sort of critical investigation of the literature that represents the standard expected of a higher-degree.

Master's and PhD level competences

Proficiency in research methods. For an MPhil, in addition to the BPhil competences discussed above, the thesis is required to demonstrate 'proficiency in the
methods and techniques of research'. Some research degree regulations word it
a little differently. For example, one says, 'Demonstrate an understanding of
research methods appropriate to the field of study.' In other words, you do not
have to be proficient in all research methods, just those of relevance to your
topic area (which, of course, makes eminent sense). Proficiency in research
methods is an important distinguishing factor for Master's level and above: you
need to show a critical understanding not only of the *results* of research undertaken in your field of study, but also of *the methods and techniques used to obtain
those results*. Furthermore, you need to show that you can apply those methods
and techniques yourself. This does not mean that you have to use every technique in the book, only that you must be able to show that you know about
them and have chosen and justified one or more methods that are most appropriate to your particular research project.

   This, and the other additional criterion discussed below, also apply to a dissertation as part of a taught Master's course, although a dissertation is obviously
far shorter than an entire Master's by thesis. Even so, it should be to the same
standard and so display the same competences. There may also be very specific
requirements, for example applying competences and techniques that were part
of the taught component of the course. If so they should be specified.

   Initiative and independence of thought. This point follows on from the issues
raised in respect of the topic review. It is about showing that you have an understanding of what you are investigating and are not treating research as a
mechanical process – even though it may involve a lot of routine work.

   It is very important to show *how* you did your research – warts and all.
Things always go wrong in any research project. How you overcame challenges
and problems shows your initiative and independence!

   A distinct contribution to scholarship. This requirement for a Master's may
sound a rather daunting prospect. It is really about showing that you have the
astuteness to sort out where you can make a useful contribution. For a PhD, the
OU regulations use the term 'a significant contribution to knowledge'. De
Montfort regulations require that a PhD will 'constitute an independent and
original contribution to knowledge'. These are both a step up from the Master's
requirement. It does not mean that the *whole* of a PhD thesis must be original
and every bit of it is a contribution to knowledge, just that there is something
original in it.

   Behind both these phrases there is the concept of originality in research.
Chapter 17 of Cryer (2000) explores this subject. First a warning for Master's
students, in that although she does say that 'all research degrees should show
originality to some extent', the chapter is written with PhD standard largely in
mind. In a Master's – and particularly in a Master's dissertation – some of the
options for expressing originality are less viable than in a PhD project. However,
the way in which Cryer explores originality is very useful.

ACTIVITY   **READING**

Read through chapter 17 of Cryer (2000) and work through the activity (pp. 195–6).

Cryer's activity asks you to look at your general field of study to consider how different developments can be viewed as original in different ways. There are many ways to fulfil the originality criterion and I could think of additions to her list. You may have even more original ideas on being original. Cryer's big point is how unpredictable originality can be. My development of her list follows, together with suggestions from some colleagues.

Originality categories

1   *A new product.* Just making something new is not academically adequate – it has to be made as a result of the research process (e.g. analysing the way in which an existing product or component undertakes a task and then demonstrating how it could be improved – scientific and engineering PhDs can be of this nature).

2   *Providing something new for the first time.* This can be anything from a new material or geological samples from an unexplored area to new social data or an archaeologist digging a new site. Again, the provision of something new must be linked with a research process. Just digging up a load of bones or discovering a new animal will not do; it needs to be set in the context of a particular archaeological or biological debate, and we need to be shown how the discovery advances understanding.

3   *A development of or an improvement on something which already exists.* Originality can be developing further a previously original piece of work.

4   *A new theory or perspective.* This can include a synthesis of existing information using the new theory/perspective by way of verification.

5   *A reinterpretation of an existing theory.* This can involve an original exposition of another's work – for example, suggesting that an alternative theoretical interpretation of data is possible that provides a better understanding of the system under study.

6   *Applying an existing idea or theory to a new field or a set of data.* For example, taking a model that was developed under lab conditions and seeing if it works with field data.

7   *A new research tool or technique.* For example, in one PhD the student applied a psychology methodology to a transport planning issue (traffic calming) and did fieldwork to test its viability. This had never been done before and the thesis established both the concept and the feasibility of doing it.

8   *A new model or perspective.* This can be anything from a new mathematical model to a new way of understanding how a key scientific idea affects research or a new commentary on a classical Latin poem.

9   *A new in-depth study.* This could add to knowledge (for example, by detailing a process already known in outline), without necessarily developing a new perspective.

10 *A critical analysis.* Showing originality in testing somebody else's idea and/or developing an original critique.

11 *A portfolio of work based on research.* In some art research degrees, in particular, a portfolio can demonstrate students' competence in their subject. A PhD by publications (usually available only to staff of a university) also involves the use of an existing portfolio of research.

12 *A collection of generalisable findings or conclusions.* In this case originality is in the generalisations made. My own thesis was of this type; it pulled together secondary information on the land use/transport design of Britain's new towns and drew comparative and generalisable conclusions about their efficiency in providing personal mobility to their residents.

13 *Carrying out original work within a project designed by others.* Laboratory and experimental PhD projects can take place within a larger team research project. The scope and design of the PhD project are thus largely predetermined. This is quite common and is accepted, but you need to ensure that your own originality plays a part as well.

These categories are not exclusive; indeed, there are quite a few overlaps. However, it is useful to develop a list like this in order to think through what constitutes originality. In many cases originality does not necessarily require generating new data or material, but is about utilising existing material in an original way. Remember that originality does not apply to the *whole* thesis or dissertation; it means only that it contains something original. For example, one student commented:

> I think what my examiners felt was original in my own PhD was that I applied systems theories to a particular area of NHS activity which had not really been investigated systematically before (performance measurement systems), and included a development of an existing process (being debated among systems academics at the time) for choosing appropriate methodologies for investigating different types of problems. A consequence of this interdisciplinarity was I needed three examiners – one expert on the performance measurement issues, one on NHS policy with a bit of systems background, and one expert on the systems approaches I'd applied!

In this case the originality was in both applying an existing method to a new area and developing the method further.

PhD level competences

Chapter 3 of Phillips and Pugh (2000) discusses the nature of a PhD and how the competences that are shared with a Master's are actually more stringent in the case of a PhD.

ACTIVITY 2.7

In which of these ways do you expect your research to be original? Or will it be original in another way? You may have only a vague or preliminary idea at the moment, but suggest what you can.
Discuss this with your supervisor as well as making your own notes in your research journal.

READING

Read the first three sections of chapter 3 (pp. 19–24 of Phillips and Pugh, 2000).

Phillips and Pugh argue that a PhD essentially needs to demonstrate that:

1   You have a command of your subject and demonstrate it by having 'something to say'.
2   You have the astuteness to sort out where you can make a useful contribution.
3   You know the methods and techniques of investigation (and their limitations).
4   You can communicate the results effectively.
5   Overall, it shows that you are a professional in your field.

As well as the requirement to make an original contribution to knowledge, which has already been considered above, Phillips and Pugh say that the key hallmark of a PhD is to demonstrate that you are a 'fully professional researcher'.

This point features in all UK university regulations, which contain some phrase indicating that a PhD should demonstrate your capacity to pursue further research without supervision. This is about arriving as a professional in your field. A PhD should show that you know how to design a research project, organise it, carry it out and report the results. In consequence it is important in your PhD to:

1   Show *how* you did your research as well as *what* you found out. (Theses are often thin on the crucial *how* side.)
2   Show warts and all – how you overcame problems. (Things always go wrong in even the best organised research project.)
3   Even if the results are negative, they can still represent an original contribution, particularly if you display a professional use of the research methods in your field.

The OU regulations contain a further criterion, which is that the PhD should contain *material worthy of publication*. This is one way of demonstrating that you have arrived in your field of research, although not all university regulations require examiners to consider whether a thesis has material of publishable quality. It should be emphasised that such a criterion does not mean that the whole thesis is worthy of publication, just that it contains something in it that is. An indisputable way to prove this is to publish papers based on your thesis work. However, do check with your supervisor or research office, as some institutions do not permit the publication of thesis chapters before a viva. Editing the material may get you round this.

What will the examiner be looking for?

Chapter 8 deals with the examination process and the viva. An examiner will be asked to report specifically on how the candidate fulfilled the specific requirements for each research degree. In summary, your examiner will be looking for the following key indicators that reflect whether you have demonstrated the competences expected for a research degree:

1   Clear focus.
2   A good grasp of the nature of the situation addressed.
3   A coherent rationale for undertaking the research.
4   Good connections with existing work on the topic.
5   The results and conclusions displayed in a scholarly and creative manner.

For a Master's or doctorate examiners will also look for:

1   A method appropriate to the topic of investigation.
2   Originality.
3   Evidence that you have 'arrived' as a professional in your field.

ACTIVITY 2.8

How would you know whether your thesis has fulfilled the academic criteria listed above for your research degree? It would be useful to discuss your response with your supervisor.

Familiarising yourself with research standards

Having given some thought to the criteria for your research degree, it could be worthwhile looking at some publications in your intended field of study in terms of how they represent good research. This could be of particular use for inexperienced researchers or part-time external research students.

Chapter 6 of Cryer (2000), 'Towards recognising quality in research', is designed to take you through a set of publications that you or your supervisor select in your research area. Look at it and discuss with your supervisor whether it would be beneficial to you to work through this chapter and its activities. Rather than doing it now, you could possibly do it as part of your topic review, when you need to be working through key publications in any case. Part of looking at the research in your field is to get an idea of the standards expected.

It is very useful to look at successful relevant dissertations or theses in your field. This should help focus on what are the standards expected. Even in a very specific topic area, theses can take varied and diverse forms, utilising different research approaches and methods. Your supervisor should be able to suggest some for you to see. You will need to read some quite thoroughly, but for others at least skim through them to get a general feel.

Remember that specific subject areas have traditions and styles of their own that cannot be covered in this book. Talk to your supervisor about this.

Transferring from MPhil to PhD

Before leaving the subject of competences required for a research degree, mention needs to be made of transferring between an MPhil and a PhD. In many universities, PhD research students are first registered for a Master's degree and then, after about nine months' study, are required to submit a transfer report to be upgraded to a PhD (see Cryer, 2000, chapter 16). The transfer report is typically 5,000–10,000 words in length and involves:

1   The completion of an initial review of the subject.
2   The identification of the research problem to be addressed.
3   The development of a research plan.

The De Montfort University regulations for a transfer report indicate that the research plan should 'include details of the original contribution to knowledge which is likely to emerge'. This indicates the key criterion that you need to demonstrate in a transfer report: that you have demonstrated the potential to achieve PhD-level competences.

As I have said, not all universities require students to prepare formal and assessed transfer reports. For example, at the Open University students are not initially registered for a specific research degree but, after a probationary period, their supervisors provide a report recommending registration for a specific research degree. They have to meet similar criteria to a transfer report, but the onus is on the supervisor to ensure that a student has met the necessary criteria for PhD-level work.

It is also increasingly the practice for students to first register for a Master's in Research Methods (MRes) and then proceed to a PhD. Again, during the MRes, you are expected to demonstrate your potential for PhD-level work, which is a key criterion in awarding the MRes itself.

ACTIVITY 2.9

If you are expecting to undertake a PhD, find out whether you have to prepare a transfer report, or what other form of review will take place towards the end of the first year of study. Note down the criteria that need to be met.

READING

Now read the second part of Cryer (2000), chapter 16 ('Transferring from MPhil to PhD') and complete her activity.

The tasks that a transfer report contains (topic review, focusing on a research question and developing a research plan) are all in this book, so whatever your regulations may be, the following chapters will equip you to face them.

Starting off

Having considered what constitutes a research degree or dissertation, the obvious question is 'How to get going?' Chapter 3 looks at the initial stages of the research process in more detail, but the following may be useful to you as an overview. It will be developed in Chapter 3, 'Planning and organising a research project'.

As was discussed in Chapter 1, research is often presented in retrospect as a linear, systematic process, moving from a general subject area to sorting out a project aim, with the student drawing upon information on the 'state of the art' to design and implement the research project.

In practice the process is full of feedback loops and, certainly to begin with, can feel quite confusing. People tend to leave this out of their written reports. Quite often, however, they admit when asked that the first few months of a research degree (and even the initial time spent on a Master's dissertation) involved a lot of sorting out what to do. Look back at Martin Le Voi's two accounts of his own PhD in Chapter 1. The first account looked very logical when he wrote it up in terms of research stages, but in truth it was far from being so – as was revealed in the second account!

Your supervisor or others may have a similar story to tell – or of other researchers in their field, even if they are unwilling to confess to such experiences themselves.

READING

At this point it would be useful to read chapter 7 of Phillips and Pugh (2000), entitled 'The PhD process'. Although it is written with a PhD-scale research project in mind, it is relevant to any research degree.

In chapter 7 Phillips and Pugh explore two main themes. First, the different moods students experience at different stages of their research projects; this point is related to the discussion above of how research never runs to plan and sometimes things can be very frustrating. It is worth recognising that such moods are very typical and they (or a variant of them) will happen to you. The authors move on to the practical aspects of planning a short- and long-term timetable to complete a piece of research and the importance of setting deadlines.

ACTIVITY 2.10

Have you experienced any of the situations mentioned by the students in the examples given? If so, note how they overcame any initial difficulties. Are there lessons for yourself?

ACTIVITY 2.11

What do you see as the key tasks to be done in the first few months of your project?

Why are these tasks so important?

How do you propose to set about these tasks?

How will you measure your success?

Sketch out a work programme of the crucial tasks you think will be involved in:

1 Over the next three months.
2 Producing the thesis as a whole.

The planning and organisation of your research project are considered in detail in Chapter 3 but, even if you alter your plans, it is worthwhile starting to sort out a rough project structure now.

Formalities and support services

Finally, in considering how you are starting your research, it is worth going through the support provided for students by your department and university.

Chapter 5 of Cryer (2000), entitled 'Settling in as a new research student' includes things like familiarising yourself with your department's facilities and services, and training provision. It would be worthwhile to work your way through this section of her chapter now. The following sections pick up and develop some of the key points in Cryer's chapter.

Departmental research training

As mentioned at the beginning of this chapter, the book covers only generic research training aspects. For training in, for example, methods specific to your subject area, your supervisor or department should advise you on what is available. Do keep in touch with other research students in your department or even others doing similar work in other institutions. You can learn most of 'the ropes' from each other. I did my PhD full-time at the Open University in its pioneering years and I was the only research student in the Social Sciences Faculty. To some extent I was facing problems of isolation similar to those of a part-time student. In consequence, my supervisor encouraged me to network with students and other researchers elsewhere, which I found to be very helpful and encouraging.

Other support for your studies

Library and computing access

Full-time students will have library and computing access, but the procedures for obtaining them, and the rules of their use, will obviously vary between institutions. It is likely that each faculty/school/department will also have its own specialist computing and information technology (IT) facilitator. For part-time external research degree students, find out what library and computing support is available. The Open University, for example, will help to negotiate access to a suitable local library and some funds are available if fees are involved.

Assistance in research funding

A very important area to sort out is what money is available to support your research. Students on a Research Council grant have monies provided to their departments for research expenses and training. Make sure you know how to claim them. You may also be able to apply for support for specific expenses (for example, an overseas conference or a field trip) from your grant funder. Internal departmental or faculty/school funds may also be available through your supervisor, who should be able to advise you on all these aspects.

The situation for external, part-time research degree students is very different. They are normally expected to be self-funding. It is thus important to make allowances in designing your research programme for any additional costs that are a consequence of your research methods. (This is considered in Chapter 3, 'Planning and organising a research project'). This is also true for full-time students if your research is likely to involve costs beyond those routinely provided.

In some cases, part-time external students can apply for a limited amount of departmental or faculty/school funds through their internal supervisor, but it should be emphasised that, even when they exist, resources are very limited. Of perhaps wider relevance, several bursary schemes are offered by educational charities, the British Council or industry. Sometimes conferences provide bursaries for student attendance. It is very worthwhile having an initial talk about the financial aspects of your research with your supervisors, who may know of such schemes.

Your research office

Finally, there is always a research office, centre or school that is responsible for administering research degree studies. Sometimes this office goes beyond an administration role and provides useful support facilities for students.

Working with your supervisor

In terms of support for your studies, the relationship you have with your supervisor(s) is utterly crucial to your whole postgraduate work and experience. This

---

READING

Both Cryer (2000) and Phillips and Pugh (2000) have chapters on the supervisor–student relationship. Although there is some overlap between them, I would recommend reading both chapters, as they approach the subject from different angles. I would suggest reading first Phillips and Pugh's chapter 8, 'How to manage your supervisor'.

ACTIVITY 2.12

When you have read chapter 8 of Phillips and Pugh, make a set of notes based on their 'action summary' points at the end of the chapter. Highlight any that you feel to be of particular relevance to you and that you need to tackle.

READING

Now move on to chapter 7 of Cryer, 'Interacting with your supervisor(s)'. You can then work through Cryer's activities on the basis of the material from both chapters. Once you have completed working through this section of Cryer, discuss it and your notes on Activity 2.12 with your supervisor(s). This is of particular importance if you have any specific issues or concerns.

is particularly so for part-time students, whose main contact will be through their supervisor(s).

Note

1   If you are registered for a research degree in an institution where the Open University validates degrees (through OU Validation Services), the regulations are the same as if you were directly registered with the Open University.

Chapter 3

Planning and Organising a Research Project

David Wield

with contributions from Lynn Ashburner; Terry Newholm,
Sue Oreszczyn, Stephen Potter, Pam Smith, Alexandra di Stefano
and Clare Tagg

After reading this chapter, you will be able to:

■ **Bound and focus your ideas about the project**

■ **Draw up a plan of attack, assigning yourself key tasks**
   and keeping a research journal

■ **Schedule your time**

■ **Set the first milestone – a presentation to your**
   supervisor

This chapter aims to get you moving from your initial research idea and preliminary research questions/hypotheses towards a preparatory, but 'do-able', detailed plan of work. After you have worked through the chapter, you should feel reasonably confident about the milestones you have set yourself in your first year of research.

We would like you, by the end of the chapter, to have planned a twenty-minute talk about your work plan, suitable for a presentation to your supervisor at a face-to-face supervision session.

The chapter starts where Chapter 2 ('Getting going') left off. In Activity 2.11 of that chapter you worked out what you saw as the key tasks in the first few months of your project. You then had to write down:

1   Why these key tasks were so important.
2   How you proposed to set about the tasks.
3   How you would measure your success.

Have you discussed with your supervisor what you saw as the key tasks in the first three months of your project? Go back to your notes. What was your supervisor's reaction? What were the results of your discussion with your supervisor? Did you make changes as a result of the feedback?

ACTIVITY 3.1

Read through your notes from Activity 2.11 of Chapter 2. Make a list of the key tasks in one column of a table and, for each task, make short notes on how you are planning to go about it. Put those notes in the second column. Keep the notes with you as you work through this section. You will use them later.

Discussion

The task list below uses as an example the PhD project of an OU student, Sally Caird, on the extent to which different types of team working affect the level of innovation in small and medium enterprises (SMEs).

Key tasks	*How to do them?*
1 Generate research questions concerning research topic (for example, research on teams and the relationship between work and innovation in SMEs)	Brainstorm, make notes, try them out on supervisors

2	Begin literature survey, by deciding preliminary sub-themes, then searching and thinking about each sub-theme, one by one	Preliminary sub-themes in the above example were: (a) SMEs; (b) innovation; and (c) team working. Student immediately realised that the sub-themes were too large, so she focused on: (a) innovation in the environment industry (in which she had a particular interest); (b) innovation and SMEs; and (c) teams in SMEs
3	Make a plan for all the years of your degree programme, based on a detailed thesis outline	Begin by making a list of major tasks
4	Make notes on appropriate method and tools	Begin by making a list of potential methods, for discussion with supervisor
5	Think about how to obtain access to SMEs	Generate a list, beginning with SMEs that have obtained a prize for innovation in the last few years

… and so on.

As a further example, Box 3.1 is a task list drawn up by Alexandra di Stefano, a doctoral student who was beginning work on organisational learning in organisations based in Milton Keynes.

Questions.   How do your tasks differ from those in Box 3.1? Why do yours differ? Is it to do with the length of your project? The type of project?

How do the notes in Box 3.1 differ from those set out for the project on team working above? There are no right or wrong task lists of this type. This one focused more on preparatory issues, getting up and running, and on reflective, thinking issues. Others may focus more on detailed operational tasks.

Bounding and focusing the idea

What I mean by bounding and focusing an idea is that many research ideas are just that – ideas. Often students have difficulties in the early stages of their research as readings and ideas can send them off in several different directions. Research ideas are a starting-off point, but ideas are not a defined project.

As soon as we start trying to do something about the ideas – for example, like working out how we might find out more about them – a whole series of sub-issues usually emerges that can fog the research topic and make it very hard to grasp. Often the idea is much too big, so that it is impossible to study with any degree of certainty. When you start to find out about the idea the topic can suddenly seem overwhelming, with too much and too vague literature, unclear methods and a bewildering mixture of theoretical perspectives. So a good idea

---

BOX 3.1 Task list of a full-time doctoral student

1   Write a position statement on my research, and review it regularly.
2   Start a research journal to record ideas, note questions, 'observe' own learning, record conversations, reflections, etc.
3   Keep it going!
4   Look at a varied set of examples of research done by others, e.g. theses, journals, papers. Make notes in journal on likes and dislikes, my preferences.
5   Put thinking time into diary.
6   Visit Vice-chancellor to test claim at induction that 'door is always open'.
7   Make a pro-forma for supervision meetings.
8   Note ways to put the research topic into operation and put them in journal as targets for achievement.
9   Explore methodologies.
10   Make a list of useful contacts, organisations, keep in journal.
11   Think about practical tasks – what needs to be done so I can work?
12   Retrain myself *not* to clean the whole house before I start doctoral work! (Is this really the best displacement activity I can think of?)

---

can come at any time, but not all ideas are amenable to research. The normal means of assessing whether an idea is researchable is to see whether we can formulate the idea into researchable questions or hypotheses that can be researched in project form.

Keeping a research journal

Since ideas, and thoughts about how to research them, can come at any time, keeping a research journal is extremely important. The student task list in Box 3.1 included several tasks that involved using a journal and Box 3.2 describes how Pam Smith, now Professor of Nursing at South Bank University, used one.

I kept a much more utilitarian record book for my PhD in materials science. It was a daily record of activity – literature surveyed, equipment ordered, people spoken to, experiments done (which were detailed in other log books) – as well as more reflective sections on ideas, problems with data, collection, lack of fit between theory and data, and monthly timetables. It is also useful to have an 'action' column on the side of each page (or some other form if your journal is electronic). Figure 3.1 shows a historic example of a research journal. It is a page from the laboratory notebook of Michael Faraday (1791–1867) where he recorded his discovery of electromagnetic induction on 29 August 1831.

BOX 3.2   Keeping a research journal

Keeping a research journal is one way of helping us focus our research by having somewhere to record ideas when we have them, compile a 'first thoughts' list, formulate researchable questions or hypotheses, state precise objectives, list and try out interview questions, set up experimental ideas, start analyses, and so on. In her PhD study of nurses, Pam Smith (1988) used advice from a key critical sociologist of the 1940s and 1950s, C. Wright Mills. He suggested that the daily routine of thinking, reading and writing a little is part of learning any intellectual craft. From Wright Mills's advice to the novice researcher, 'On intellectual craftsmanship', the following extracts seemed particularly relevant.

> Any working social scientist who is well on his [sic] way ought at all times to have so many plans, which is to say ideas, that the question is always, which of them am I/ought I to work on next? And he should keep a special little file for his master agenda, which he writes and rewrites just for himself and perhaps for discussion with friends. From time to time he ought to review this very carefully and purposefully and sometimes too when he is relaxed. (Wright Mills, 1978, p. 218).

Wright Mills tells the new student, 'You must learn to use your life experience in your intellectual work continually to examine and interpret it.' He recommends that the way to do this is to keep a journal which enables the researcher 'to control this rather elaborate interplay to capture what you experience and sort it out; only in this way can you hope to guide and test your reflection' (p. 216). Smith found the extract on 'life experience' pertinent to her own situation, 'since former experiences as a nurse and nurse teacher were inevitably brought to bear on the study and indeed set the original formulation of the research problem – on the issue of the relationship between classroom and ward in nurse training – in motion. Similarly, as feminist sociologists emphasise, the gender of the researcher is also part of the fundamental experience that shapes the research enterprise. In terms of keeping a journal, Smith kept a fieldwork diary not only to capture insights about the research but also to document other events external to the research which affected her reflectivity.

The extract below is from Smith's journal, in which she discusses possible research interests and the current factors which influenced her thinking. These factors included concern about the literature, and about national and local concern with the quality of nursing care and nurse education.

> [It was the early 1980s. I was working as a nurse teacher in a care-of-the-elderly hospital (actually it was still called 'geriatrics' at the time). I was struck how variable the students' experiences were, depending on which ward they had been allocated to. I commenced my journal in March 1983, and I began by looking at the relationship between students' educational needs and ward practice. I wrote:]

Fundamental questions: how much does ward practice reflect classroom teaching? How realistic is classroom teaching in relation to practice? Is there a conflict between the two? If there is a conflict, how do students experience that conflict?

Learners frequently complain about the ideal and reality of classroom and ward. I ask them to give me some examples. They mention the Norton pressure sore risk calculator which we teach them to use in the school and is never used on the ward.

Even little things like bed making – how in the classroom they're taught to put a tuck in the blanket to give patients room to move their feet, but this again is rejected by ward staff as impractical. They also feel awkward talking to patients even though we spend a lot of time in class discussing communication and interpersonal relationships. As for the nursing process, ward staff say there is neither time nor sufficient staffing for patient allocation. It seems important to try to unravel why there is this discrepancy. Ward staff must have their reasons? In the meantime students are caught in the middle of a seemingly impossible dream.

The head of the nursing school is concerned because she is expecting a GNC [General Nursing Council] visit in the near future and there is much written in the nursing press about proposed changes in nurse education in the next few years. Students in this school of nursing get a lot of responsibility very early too and they experience great anxiety if they're having to implement ward policy they don't agree with. Need to look at Isabel Menzies' study to check how she thought student nurses managed anxiety.

Someone told me about Anna Dodds' thesis, an in-depth qualitative study which looked at student nurses' ward learning experiences. They seem to have had a really rough time. There are also a couple of recent studies which examine ward learning and the ward sister's role. They also develop characteristics of the good and less good ward learning environments. Must get hold of these.

Focusing

Developing a researchable question and/or hypothesis puts into operation and links abstract ideas from experience, theory and literature into the empirical world of data collection – meaning data in the broadest sense. In formulating researchable questions we are examining the very nature of ideas and where they come from; we are examining the relationship between ideas, research questions, approaches and methods and the paradigms on which they are based. Thus the research question or hypothesis forms an important bridge between the theory and practice of research. Because the researchable question or hypothesis has such power to link the different parts of a research project (it determines the research approach, the literature, the data collection and analysis, for example),

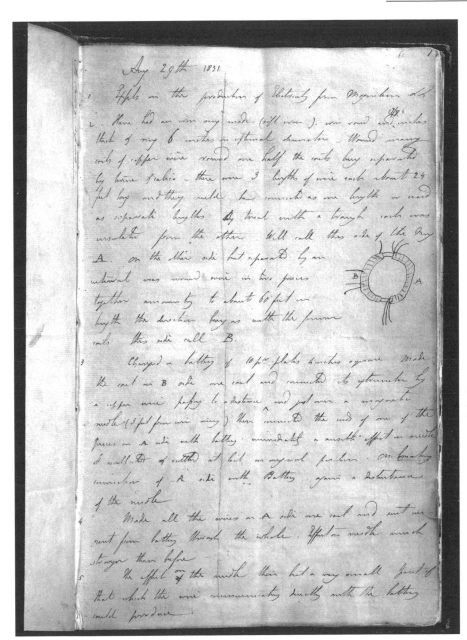

FIGURE 3.1
A page
from the
laboratory
notebook
in which
Michael
Faraday
(1791–1867)
recorded his
discovery of
electro-
magnetic
induction, 29
August 1831.
*Royal
Institution/
Bridgeman
Art Library*

I believe that formulating the researchable question or hypothesis is the most important stage of the research project. It follows that getting it right, or anything like right, will not happen immediately. But experience suggests that puzzling away at it from the beginning is the way to build confidence that your research is 'do-able'.

As you learned in Chapters 1–2, research is sometimes portrayed as a very linear process. First you have your subject area – the broad area in which you are interested. You read around on this and talk to some people and focus down on a topic area. The focus becomes narrower; then, reading and discussing your topic area more deeply, you explore a series of interesting issues and from them select your project aim, which may be in the form of a 'core question' or hypothesis. Everything then flows from that. You sort out what information is needed to provide the answer to the core question, what method(s) need to be used, and you go out and do it.

In practice there are feedback loops everywhere. Formulating your researchable question or hypothesis in anything like a workable form is unlikely to happen immediately. Each stage of the research work will result in challenging a project's focus and lead to some re-evaluation. At all times you will find that you have to maintain a careful balancing act between the desirable and the practical. Too strong a focus early on may lead to you ignoring what actually are more important issues than the one you have chosen. Too weak a focus results in following up each side issue as it emerges and not getting anywhere! So focus needs to remain an issue as the research progresses in order to avoid the pitfalls of these extremes. This may seem disconcerting, but it is a necessary feature of any good research project.

In Box 3.3 a research student, Lynn Ashburner, reflects on how her PhD project achieved focus. Lynn started from having a wide topic area (the impact of microelectronics in the service sector) and an idea (gender as an important factor that other researchers had ignored). Note how she started thinking about doing too much. She ended up narrowing down to a research question that retained her central interest in the gender idea and also fitted in with her own motivations for taking a research degree ('I felt I might influence the treatment

---

BOX 3.3   A research student's experience of focusing

I began my PhD research with little idea as to what would be studied or where. I was a student linked with a project which was looking at applications of new technology. It was studying branch banking, retailing and hospital laboratories. Having read some of the project's reports, I felt that they lacked a gender analysis. My MA dissertation had begun by looking at technology as it related to the increasing rate of unemployment and it had soon become clear that the effects of the application of new technology could not be fully understood unless gender was a central concept. My supervisor told me that I had a free hand in my thesis focus. I began to explore the literature and current research in the three wider areas of the health service, retailing and the finance sector.

The first question, as I saw it, was whether to do research that built upon previous work done or to begin something new. There is a terrible fear at this stage of the research that all you will end up with is a pale reflection of what has gone before. I felt that I wanted to try for originality in all three areas: questions asked, area chosen, and approach. The latter was the most difficult, since qualitative research and the case study approach were fairly common. What I tried to do was to set it in a quantitative context. The research questions that I addressed seemed original when I started but I was continually dismayed when other work was published that appeared to be trying to do exactly the same as mine. It was never exactly the same, however, and it was clear that the need for the approach had been generally recognised. That left the choice of research location.

There was so much research going on in the health service and there was already a large group of sociologists who specialised in that area, so with no background I decided to leave well alone. Retailing was an attractive option, since there were applications of new technology in many areas, and I explored several avenues from supermarkets to home shopping catalogues. Talks with USDAW [trade union] researchers showed that there was awareness of the possible impacts and some work had begun. I felt that the shopping catalogue sector would be interesting. There were large numbers of women employees usually in jobs which were segregated from those of male employees. They were also largely seen as unskilled or semi-skilled.

At that time there had been little research on gender and a growing amount on women workers. When looking at certain occupations this divide became inevitable, given the extent of gender segregation. I wanted to look at both men and women in the same jobs to see what was gender-specific about the processes which affected men and women's work when new technology was introduced. I was thus drawn to banking, since there was already a strong base of research on new technology in this area as well as some work on gender. Indeed, the extent of research in progress was a possible disadvantage. Research in insurance was then sparse but I was aware of several ongoing projects. I turned to consideration of building societies. There were a large number of parallels with the operations within banking and I felt that I could use the banking research to inform my own. The percentage of women in the sector was considerably higher than in banking or insurance and the image of building societies as 'friendly' institutions meant that they were not seen [as] as 'high-powered' as banks and I felt that this might influence the treatment and prospects of women employees.

The more I investigated this option the more the pieces seemed to slot into place and the clearer I could see the research questions emerging. Although the focusing and refinement of the project continued into the data collection stage and beyond there were clear signs that, although I knew absolutely nothing about building societies or the labour process that existed within them, there was the potential for an interesting piece of research, as most of the requirements of my theoretical perspective could be met. Women and men could be found in the same jobs at all stages within the branch networks and in this sense women were not necessarily confined to the lower-skilled work. There were opportunities to take professional examinations. The majority of research on women workers had been done in the manufacturing sector and there was very little looking at female white-collar workers. This sector was unusual in that there was little or no trade union representation. This meant that employers could make decisions on computerisation without such potential restraints.

There were other factors that influenced my choice of focus. The functions of building societies, prior to the 1987 legislation, were very limited and I felt that this would reduce the number of variables and thus greatly facilitate the comparison of developments between societies. I also decided to look only at branch work because developments within head offices involved computer applications that were common to most office environments. The development of computerisation in the branches went beyond the holding and transmission of data and involved the mechanisation of a wide range of manual tasks. This sector was experiencing considerable growth and had been little affected by the recession, resulting in very few redundancies. Therefore possible job losses were not influencing people's perceptions of the processes at work. By confining the case studies to building society branches there was a clear 'boundary' which could be drawn round the numbers of people to be interviewed. On top of all this I could not find any research or ongoing work which was looking at the labour process within building societies. This at least might be my claim to originality!

and prospects of women employees'). Also note that, as the focus on a researchable question emerged, so too did a focus on method.

Box 3.4 is another example of a research student from a different discipline focusing on their research topic. In this case, from a vast possibility of research into neural networks, the student (David Bradbury) incrementally narrowed the field of possibilities down to a sub-area with a manageable literature, which then allowed the identification of a specific project for which the current state of research was almost 'crying out'. Note that the student picked up one of the issues identified in Chapter 5 on the purposes of a topic review: there was parallel work that had not been linked and this provided the crucial focusing element for the thesis.

Thus David Bradbury's idea was that integrating isolated work could form the basis of a project. This idea did indeed have the potential to be defined in terms of specific objectives and tasks and made a good, well focused project. David pursued the comparative project, developed it further as a result of infor-

BOX 3.4   Focusing on neural networks

The chosen topic area is the use of neural networks in cognitive modelling. Neural networks are flavour of the month and have attracted hoards of researchers from all over the world and from all disciplines. Meetings of the International Neural Network Society attract literally thousands of attenders. With such a bemusing range of research, focusing on a particular project is hard going: the number of journals, technical reports and conference proceedings is itself daunting.

The student did a literature search and began to get interested in the area of recurrent neural networks. (Recurrent networks, unlike non-recurrent types, allow connections from individual 'neurons' to others in the same layer.) This seemed relatively new and had smaller numbers of workers in the field, making it easier to think of a project which had not been done before. Some recent work indicated that about four or five algorithms and architectures for learning had been developed. At this point it became clear that the individual projects which had developed these algorithms had been working with no attempt at integrating or comparing their models with the others, since the work in each area was so new that mostly they had not come across each other.

The student identified an opportunity to do a comparative study of several different approaches to learning in recurrent neural networks. The study could use head-to-head comparison of the algorithms and architectures on carefully chosen learning tasks, allowing meaningful comparisons of performance, strengths and weaknesses to be identified that were not just task-specific, nor restricted to one or two approaches at once.

mation that came in and new work that was published while he was working, and managed to finish within four years.

Research questions

I am going to spend some time working through the generation of research questions and hypotheses. First, though, here is a simple but important tip. One good way of making sense of a research idea or research topic is to think of it as a project with a definite time limit. Such a project will produce, synthesise and analyse data into your thesis. This may seem very simple, simplistic even, but it is surprising how many prospective research students lose track of the project nature of their work with the result that it spins out of control. That is why, in this section, we are looking at four issues that emerge as you develop your project. The first is one of focus (or bounding), followed by work plans, time management, and setting milestones.

Focus or bounding

Discussion

A well known hypothesis in health science and health policy is: smoking causes cancer.

In environmental science an interesting hypothesis is: global warming is a natural phenomenon unaffected by human fossil fuel consumption.

A hypothesis that could have been generated for the research topic on team work and innovation in SMEs (Activity 3.1) might have been: team working improves innovation in small and medium enterprises.

A hypothesis that is well known in economic and political science is: British industry is short-termist.

These hypotheses could be turned into research questions, simply, as follows:

1   Does smoking cause cancer?
2   Does human fossil fuel consumption cause global warming?
3   Does team working improve innovation in SMEs?
4   Is British industry short-termist?

So far, so good; these may seem to be reasonable hypotheses and questions. The next step is to work on whether they are researchable and soon I will ask you to work on tightening up your questions or hypotheses.

Research questions are a set of defined questions that a researcher wants to explore, setting priorities and focuses of attention, thus excluding a range of unstudied topics. Research questions are usually refined so that they implicitly or explicitly represent a conceptual framework and a means of putting into operation. The wording of the question determines the focus and scope of the study (Morse, 1994, p. 226). As was suggested above, the researchable question directs the literature review, the framework of study, data collection, and the analysis and write-up. As Morse emphasises, the research focus can be rather tenuous in the early stages of research. Clearly, the search for a research question is likely to be a lengthy process involving a series of iterations. Although initial formulations of research questions will probably lack a clear focus, through a narrowing process, thinking hard about theory and information or data collection possibilities, the improved question, or questions, will be more researchable and yield clearer and more important answers. In arriving at research questions the researcher generally does not 'start from scratch' but has the benefit of sources of information that may be useful in the development of research questions. These sources include existing theory on the topic, previous research, the beliefs and experiences of colleagues who have an interest in the topic area, and your own beliefs, experiences and insights. Using these sources will aid the formulation of improved research questions.

To summarise, the core research question needs to:

1   Be convertible into tasks for a research project.
2   Have a comparative element (over time, between groups, with a standard).
3   Let you know when you have done enough for an answer (i.e. is not too vague).
4   Specify the:

   (a) Field of study.
   (b) Limits of the 'population' (geographical area, industrial sector, type of specimen, etc.).
   (c) Unit of analysis.
   (d) Measures used.

5   Have theoretical links with big questions in the subject area in general. (Although you cannot do the whole picture in your project, but only one bit of the jigsaw, you can say how your bit contributes to understanding the whole.)

What are the characteristics of good research questions? What follows is not intended to be complete, but merely to give a few thoughts from people with experience. First, the question should be personally interesting to you, since you will be working on it for quite some time. If the topic does not 'grab you' it is unlikely to keep your enthusiasm to the end. Second, good research questions are likely to come from your experience or interest. Third, there usually need to be a few key concepts which can be thought about in terms of indicators. This last characteristic is not immediately apparent to researchers as they develop researchable questions. Although such putting into operation through hard-thought-out concepts and 'measures' (quantitative or qualitative) will not immediately yield an acceptable research project plan, it is important to have some confidence that the research is 'do-able'. One doctoral student came to his supervisors with three related ideas after two weeks. His supervisors suggested that, instead of trying to pull them all together in a chaotic mess, he should go away and think hard about how researchable each question was. It took about one month for this work, but after that the student continued with the chosen question for the three years to PhD submission.

Describing a research problem involves selection. What we select is determined by what we believe to be relevant to our requirements. For example, a problem of low productivity among a group of employees may be amenable to several approaches. A production engineer might tackle the problem by study-ing the work flow, work methods, etc., whilst an industrial psychologist might think a study of work-group norms or management leadership styles relevant to a solution. So whenever we tackle a problem we are making a decision – a choice is made between a range of possible aspects and interpretations.

In order to describe a problem we need to define our terms and think of ways of avoiding imprecision or lack of definition of many commonly used terms. I am sure that you will have experienced discussions in which people are using identi-cal words to mean completely different things. The researcher has to define the variable or concept of interest more precisely, usually in a way that permits mea-surement or at least ensures that the reported observations are unambiguous. Definition determines how we classify objects, abstract concepts and people.

The importance of definition is illustrated in the following dialogue, quoted in Murdick and Cooper (1982, p. 21). Russell Ackoff, a well known US-based systems and management thinker, was asked to determine the precision of the results of a survey designed to determine the number of rooms in dwelling units. 'Room' had not been explicitly defined and Ackoff asked what definition the survey designers had implicitly used. The conversation went thus:

'A room is a space enclosed by four walls, a floor, and a ceiling.'

The author (Ackoff) asked, 'Can't a room be triangular?'

'Sure. It can have three or four walls.'

'What about a circular room?'

'Well, it can have one or more walls.'

'What about a paper carton?'

'A room has to be large enough for human occupancy.'

'What about a closet?'

'It must be used for normal living purposes.'

'What are "normal living purposes"?'

'Look, we don't have to go through this nonsense: our results are good enough for our purposes.'

'What were your purposes?'

'To get an index of living conditions by finding the number of persons per room in dwelling units.'

'Doesn't the size of the room matter?'

'Yes, we probably should have used "square feet" of floor space, but that would have been too hard to get.'

'Doesn't the height of the room matter?'

'I guess so. Ideally, we should have used volume.'

'Would a room with ten square feet of floor area and sixty feet high be the same as one with sixty square feet of floor area and ten feet high?'

'Look, the index is good enough for the people who use it.'

'What do they use it for?'

'I'm not sure, but we've had no complaints.'

Morse (1994, p. 220) makes some excellent points about working through research question identification. She says:

> New investigators can best identify such a topic by reflecting on what is of real personal interest to them. Surprisingly, these topics may not be among those on which an individual has already written. Enticing topics may be those that distract a person in the library; they may be topics that preoccupy a person and draw him or her into interesting conversations with others. ... The topic identified may be an area of interest rather than a narrowly defined problem or question per se, and, at this stage, it is almost never an elegantly worded research question.

She goes on (p. 221):

> researchable questions often become apparent when one reads the literature. For instance, a student interested in breast-feeding may be seeking information to assist mothers coping with breast expression and find that the information in the literature consists entirely of prescriptive accounts on how to express the breasts, or maintain lactation. The discovery of a gap, of instances where no information is available, is an exciting indicator that a topic would be a good candidate for qualitative study. Similarly, if the reader has a hunch that the information available is poor or biased, or that the theory is wrong, then a qualitative study may also be indicated.

Morse is discussing qualitative research but, whether the research is to be qualitative or quantitative, or both, the two issues she mentions are key, and are not by any means apparent to a new researcher. Most new researchers read the literature to find out what is known about the subject. Morse is underlining the importance also of looking for gaps in the literature, and looking for weak data or theories that do not seem to fit with experience.

Morse also has a further helpful insight when she suggests (p. 223) that researchers should imagine what they want to find out – imagine the research outcome:

> By projecting the research outcome, the researcher may begin to conceptualise the question, the sample size, the feasibility of the study, the data sources, and so forth. A variation of this exercise may be demonstrated in the classroom: a topic of interest may be suggested and the students walked through steps in the research process, examining, in particular, the different results that would be obtained

with different questions and different strategies. For instance, consider a mock project with the title 'Arrivals and Departures: Patterns of Human Attachment'. We could imagine we are studying human attachment at the local airport, watching passengers leave relatives or be greeted by relatives. Then, by listing various questions that would be best asked using different qualitative strategies, we quickly discover the differences in the main types of qualitative strategies. Students can participate in these hypothetical research projects by imagining who would be best to interview as participants in each project, or, if an observational method is selected for discussion, where and when the observations could be conducted. Students can explore issues of sample size and modes of data analysis ... This type of 'planning' is crucial to the development of a solid and enticing proposal. The mental walk-through that the researcher takes in envisioning research plans may even ease some of the researcher anxiety that is invariably a part of entering the setting.

Research hypotheses

Research questions can be further focused into *hypotheses*, although this is not a universal trend. A hypothesis usually makes a statement about a relationship between variables. Verma and Beard (1981, p. 184) define a hypothesis as

> *a tentative proposition which is subject to verification through subsequent investigation. It may also be seen as a guide to the researcher in that it depicts and describes the method to be followed in studying the problem. In many cases hypotheses are hunches that the researcher has about the existence of relationships between variables.*

Hypotheses mostly make statements about relations between variables and provide the researcher with a guide as to how the original hunch might be tested. If we hypothesise, because experience suggests it may be so, that team working (one variable) has an influence on innovation (another variable), we can attempt to find out whether it is so.

A hypothesis differs from a problem statement in several ways. A problem asks a question about the relationship between variables or events, that is, how they are related to one another, whereas a hypothesis offers a tentative answer to the question. The hypothesis translates the problem into forms that facilitate testing of the relationship by methods of statistical inference. For example, the question 'How are managers' rewards related to size of organisation?' can be translated into the proposition (hypothesis): 'Rewards (defined in some measurable way) are greater the larger the organisation (again defined in a way to facilitate measurement).'

Moreover a hypothesis provides a more specific guide to research than a problem statement. Indeed, a most important role for a hypothesis is that it guides the direction of the study. A common problem in research is the proliferation of interesting information. The hypothesis helps a researcher to keep to the relevant areas by guiding and limiting what shall be studied and what shall not. Identifying which items are relevant and which are not will indicate what form of research design is likely to be the most appropriate. It also provides a framework for organising the conclusions that result from the study.

What is a 'good' hypothesis? A good hypothesis should fulfil a number of conditions. Stone (1987) suggests the following criteria.

1   The variables used in a hypothesis should all have empirical counterparts, that is, there should be a way of observing or 'creating' such a variable.
2   A hypothesis should provide an answer (albeit tentatively) to the question raised by the problem statement.
3   A hypothesis should be as simple as possible. One hypothesis is simpler than another if it refers to a smaller number of independent elements.

You may not have enough information on your problem to move from research questions to hypotheses. Your project will then become more descriptive and will be in danger of failing to answer any of the 'Why?' questions. However, a well executed exploratory project on whether there is any relationship between certain constructs could be successful.

There are different approaches to these key activities of generating research questions and hypotheses. In Activity 3.3 you will read an extract from a classic text which gives a simple summary of research questions and their relation to characteristics and types of research.

ACTIVITY 3.3

Look at the research questions or hypotheses you have generated for your research topic. Remind yourself of what you have done so far. Then read pp. 46–51 of the set book by Phillips and Pugh (up to the section 'Which type of research for the PhD?') in which they summarise some of the characteristics and types of research. After reading the extract, revisit your questions or hypotheses. Have you generated questions or hypotheses or both? If you have generated only hypotheses, try developing questions. If you have generated questions, are they 'What?', 'Why?', 'How?' or 'How many?' questions? Try developing different types of question. Then try developing hypotheses from your questions.

ACTIVITY 3.4

Turn back to your two columns on 'tasks' in Activity 3.1. Do the tasks still look reasonable in the light of your work so far in this chapter?

Discussion

Regular work on your research questions or hypotheses is important as you begin to turn them into a work plan. As you change focus from research questions or hypotheses to the various tasks needed to begin research such as a literature survey or selection of method, the different strands can get 'out of sync'. Taking stock every month or so is an important way of making sure that you are not heading away from your main area of interest.

Three recent projects

To finish this section I want to use three recent projects to give an idea of how students have gradually worked on their projects. One example, referred to on p. 36, is the research of Sally Caird. She wanted to work on innovation in small and medium enterprises. Gradually she narrowed down her focus to 'team working in small and medium enterprises', and instead of looking at innovation in general she focused on SMEs that had produced environmental innovations. She was then faced with the problem of finding some such enterprises with different organisational styles. She used several sources to find around thirty enterprises. In particular, she contacted institutions which give prizes for innovation, such as the Engineering Council and the Queen's Award. Another student, Terry Newholm, had early ideas that he later focused on (see Box 3.5).

BOX 3.5   Ethical consumer study

I am doing case studies of ethical consumers and how they make decisions to purchase in what seem daunting circumstances. I started off thinking I needed lots of detailed case studies – thirty or more. To attract thirty people to become involved in in-depth study will be difficult, I thought. After all, returns on simple, low-commitment things like questionnaires are very low; how much lower where I would be asking them for lots of time and involvement.

I made ample preparations for mass circulation to attract my respondents in a series of cities/towns. In the first city where I tried to make contacts I had almost as many positive replies as I wanted in total! The key factor I'd missed was that people were highly committed to their ethical consuming and would transfer that commitment to anything which looked as if it would forward their cause. In other studies I have done people were too busy or just far less interested; it is as well to make an initial assessment. I have a thin layer of dust on a pile of neatly produced initial contact documents beside my desk.

And then my supervisor began to question the number of cases I proposed. He knew that I would not be able to complete and analyse thirty detailed cases in the time available. I said maybe I should be aiming at twenty. More important, he asked why I had chosen thirty and not twenty. Because I want lots, of course.

To test my theory we decided that three distinct groups of three case studies would be satisfactory – around ten in each location. In fact, I am now in touch with fourteen people (in Sheffield) and some, although I think not many, may drop out. I shall ensure that I have three distinct cases by contacting others from my list as necessary, weighing up the importance of thirty against the time and labour practicalities. The original megalomania was reduced for both practical and theoretical reasons but without reducing the rigour of my method.

My final example of how students have taken their research question or hypothesis and attempted to organise their research uses a much more developed 'story of a thesis'. In fact, it uses material from a paper by a student (Tagg, 1996), which was commended as the most innovative paper at a major conference. I am using this very sophisticated story because the student, Clare Tagg, found that she needed to make a personal paradigm shift and associated major methodology changes in her thesis plan. Such dramatic changes are not usual, you will be pleased to know. But they do happen and I feel that you should be aware of their existence, even though I want to emphasise that they are not common.

The second reason for including this example is that it is a very articulate presentation of methodological diversity, and a good analysis of a clash of knowledge systems – epistemologies. In this course we aim, as a minimum, to show that there is a wide range of different ways of building understanding as you conduct your research project.

BOX 3.6   Software development as a human activity

This is the story of my PhD and the effects that research method had. It is written with hindsight. The overwhelming influence at the start of my research was positivist; my first degree is in Mathematics and my second in Computer Science. The dissertation for my MSc project was very much in the tradition of computer science research.

I came to software development with both long-term practical experience and a theoretical background. I worked for ten years for the Bank of England, based first in a user department and then in professional systems development. Since then I have been a consultant developing software and helping other people to develop software. I lecture in Computer Science at the University of Hertfordshire and have supervised many computer science student projects at undergraduate and postgraduate level.

My research topic grew out of this combination of practical and theoretical experience. There appeared to be a mismatch between the issues that seemed important in my consultancy work and the subjects we were teaching in computer science. While at the university I would hotly debate the virtues of structured versus object-oriented methods or the benefits of C++ over Ada, the consultancy work seemed to centre around people. For example, in one case the approaches used in development depended on the expertise and ability of the development staff, and the success of the project depended on convincing the manager of the users that the system was not 'stupid'. The first title of my research was consequently 'Software development is more than method' and I sought to demonstrate that, even if you get the method and tools right, there are other important considerations.

For my PhD I registered at the Open University Business School in order to give me a different perspective on the problems of software development. In keeping with the research traditions of the disciplines, research method was more of an issue at the Business School than in the Division of Computer Science, where I was lecturing, but in both departments a positivist outlook prevailed.

Theory informed by data

In the first year of research, my concerns were mainly with theory and the difficulty of handling diverse theory as I investigated the literature in order to define what it means to 'get the method and tools right'. At that stage I saw research method as unimportant, uninteresting or irrelevant and, although I was reading many of the sources I subsequently cited in my thesis, I did not make sense of what I was reading. I have to confess that I found the arguments about research philosophy a distracting side issue.

I recognised early on the importance of following particular cases through time. My own experience indicated that the impact of the decisions and factors influencing systems development was often apparent only after the system had been implemented (maybe years later). I searched for a research method based on longitudinal studies but there is little literature about longitudinal studies of information systems development, and literature from the social sciences seemed irrelevant because of its emphasis on individuals rather than organisations.

From reading the literature on science and scientific method, I adopted a positivist research strategy. The framework was to be derived from the literature and informed by a few rich longitudinal studies to provide examples and enable hypotheses to be tested within a feedback loop.

Taking this feedback approach, I began to read widely from the management, the information systems and the computer science literatures. It was soon apparent that I was going to be swamped by the volume and diversity of the material. To assist with the process of building the framework, I turned to mind mapping to facilitate the innovating structuring of information that is part of research.

During this period I was beginning to think about the longitudinal cases that were to inform the theory in the feedback loop. The first case was C, the consultancy project which had provided the impetus for the research. My consultancy was mainly concerned with supporting the project manager who had no experience of developing software systems.

To address the issue of why a piece of software is built, and to pilot the approach to be taken in the longitudinal cases, I became involved with T, a small manufacturing business which makes high-quality bespoke furniture and specialist joinery. The management did not use a computer but were considering buying a lap-top and agreed to become a case study for my research, provided I gave them advice about which computer system to buy!

In discussing the case it was noticeable that my verbal descriptions were much richer than my written notes and that important contextual information had been lost in the writing. I also realised that I was losing a lot of the flavour of the case by using my own words rather than those of the partners.

My third case was completely different. G is a subsidiary of a large insurance company. It was in the process of having an internationally distributed database built for it by the IT function at head office. At the start of the study the first phase had just gone live. On the advice of my supervisors, I taped the conversations I had at G. I found that I had to take a much more passive role than in the previous two cases because of the size and complexity of the system.

Data informed by theory

After six months of serious data collection, with the three new cases fully under way, I began to become overwhelmed with the data. At this point, chance played a part. I finally acquired a copy of Dey's book on qualitative data analysis (1993). What I found was a structured, organised approach to the analysis of qualitative data. This was the beginning of a year spent trying to make sense of the literature on qualitative research.

It soon became clear that qualitative research means more than the analysis of non-numeric data, although this was my starting point. Moreover, qualitative research means such different things to different people that it was hard coming to the literature for the first time. The terminology is foreign, writers are often bent on describing what they are not (positivist) rather than what they are, and terminology depends on the discipline. During this year I joined the electronic discussion list QUALRS_L and the discussions on the list determined my reading.

Three important interrelated strands emerged which shaped the final research approach.

Within the *methodological* strand, the concern for method or how the research was to be conducted was gradually overlaid by an awareness that it cannot be separated from the underlying ontological and epistemological beliefs. So, for example, when using case studies in research, the way in which the data are to be used to generate or support theory affects the choice of case study and the way in which it is conducted.

The *ontological* strand was characterised by considerations of what is worth knowing. The initial hypothesis – 'the process of software development depends on more than the methods, tools and techniques which are the traditional concerns of computer scientists' – was replaced by the much more open-minded research question 'If software development is viewed as a human activity, what emerges?'

Intertwined with these concerns were *epistemological* issues of appropriate ways of addressing the research question. Initially, as reflected by the action-research approach, there was an emphasis on identifying causal relationships. This was replaced by acceptance of the value of studying the world as it is, which is reflected in the change in emphasis between theory and data.

Developing a research paradigm

The holistic world view indicated by the previous section in which theory is generated from data collection indicated that a qualitative approach to the research should be adopted. Additional indicators were the difficulty of justifying the existence of objective reality when palpably users and software people see things differently and the absence of a well understood core theory on which the research could be based.

During this period the research question was further refined to be: 'What are the key themes of software development?' A detailed method of analysis and synthesis supported by a software package emerged from this period. A significant factor in the methodological considerations was the issue of quality. The criteria for judging quality research had to be established on the basis of arguments presented in the literature combined with considerations of the research audiences.

Analysing the data

Throughout year 3 I was still collecting data for all five of my longitudinal studies and ended up with many pages of documents and notes and hours of taped conversations for each case. I decided to concentrate on the detailed analysis of one case, G. From the start of using a tape recorder I had problems with transcription. For a long time I believed that I could manage with my notes, transcribing only those parts of the conversations that I needed. I finally resolved to transcribe the twenty-nine hours of tapes of case G myself.

Comment

Having retold my story, I am no longer amazed that I became daunted by the process. With the benefit of hindsight, some key issues arising from this story, I think, are:

1 Qualitative research is important in information systems research because of the rich insights it provides into problems which are not well understood.

The key issues in software development emerging from my research are accepted as critically important by practitioners and yet are not addressed in the academic literature in any coherent manner.

2 Doing qualitative research well is more than adopting a different research method; it involves a reappraisal of the paradigm of research, which has significant impacts on all aspects of the PhD process. This includes the nature of the research question, the way in which data are collected and analysed and how the results are presented.

3 For qualitative PhDs to become commonplace in information systems, there is a need for a more in-depth understanding of the issues among supervisors and examiners. A number of recent events have served to raise consciousness of alternative paradigms but without detailed, practical experience is it possible to guide a PhD student through the quagmire?

Conclusion

If I had my time again, what would I do differently? I do not regret the turn my research has taken. It has opened up to me the whole field of qualitative research and this has become an important element of my working life. I also feel that I am part of the move to increase the use and respectability of qualitative approaches in more scientific disciplines.

As you reflect on this section and the process of focusing and bounding your project, you might remember when you start to present your research not to forget to explain the focus of your project, justify it (and any changes), and show how your method of investigation stems from your core question. An important part of an academic research project is showing you know how to undertake the process of research, not just reporting the results.

Towards a work plan

It is often said that there are three key reasons why students experience difficulty in research projects. The first is selecting a 'suitable' topic – one where it is possible to 'find out' without trying to do too much. The previous section discussed this issue in some detail. The second reason is selecting an appropriate analytical framework – a means by which understanding can be enhanced. The third difficulty, which I want to introduce now, is inability to manage resources, particularly time.

The first three months are key in the planning of the whole research period. It is possible, if enough time is given to it in the first three months, to make a reasonable plan for the whole project. Obviously the later periods will not be as well mapped out as the earlier ones but it is crucial that the whole period is mapped out, with stages. Below is a schema (adapted from Murray,

1996, p. 5) that includes some of the obvious steps in the research process. They can be added to by individual students. You already have your task list, which will differ from this list in many respects but can be used to construct a year plan. The tasks in italics indicate where writing is required. I have emphasised the need to write because it is often put off when, in fact, it is needed right from the beginning. The subject of Chapter 4 is 'The writing process'.

1   *Year 1*
    Research proposal and mission statement.
    Literature review (or state-of-the-art review).
    Choosing a bibliographic system/package.
    Setting up a meeting system and schedule.
    Keeping records/research journal.
    Plan the whole research period and process.
    Investigate similar research theses done by others.
    Attend relevant courses.
    Develop research questions/hypotheses.
    Plan for access to research and/or equipment.
    Begin developing methods.
    First-year report.
    Feedback and adjust second-year plan.
2   *Year 2*
    Develop method.
    Design and conduct experiments.
    Begin analysis.
    Continue ideas log book and work research journal.
    Start drafting chapters.
    Keep record of readings.
    Adapt meeting style.
    Review plan.
    Second-year report.
    Seek feedback.
    Respond to feedback.
3   *Year 3*
    Update reading.
    Complete analysis.
    Complete experiments.
    Interpret results.
    Develop recommendations.
    Complete chapter drafts.
    Seek feedback.
    Respond to feedback.

As Buchanan (1980, pp. 45–8) points out, the typical stages of a research project can easily be identified. He divides the research process into three broad phases: deciding what to do, doing it, and communicating what has been done:

1   Deciding what to do:

    (a) Decide topic.
    (b) Define objectives.
    (c) Choose methodology.
    (d) Obtain information sources.

2   Doing it:

    (a) Collect data.
    (b) Analyse data.

3   Communicating what has been done:

    (a) Develop conclusions.
    (b) Develop recommendations.
    (c) Notify organisation, or source of information, of findings.

Research in practice is seldom as easy and straightforward as this sequential pattern implies. You may go through the procedure several times and overlap in your work across the phases. There are likely to be many parallel activities. Moreover, research always involves an element of risk and uncertainty and you can never be sure that all the information will be available. Some projects may have to be revised or even discarded because of inadequate information, and you may have to start again. Careful selection of your topic may have mitigated some of the risk and uncertainty inherent in a project, but there is still the problem of managing available resources, especially your time. Hence the first essential is to plan and effectively manage your research activities.

The major purposes of such planning are given by Howard and Sharp (1989, p. 47) as to:

1   Clarify the aims and objectives of the researcher.
2   Define the activities required to attain these aims and the order in which they take place.
3   Identify various critical points or 'milestones' in the research at which progress can be reviewed and the research plan reassessed.
4   Produce estimates of times at which the various milestones will be reached so that progress can be clearly measured.
5   Ensure that effective use is made of the key resources, particularly the researcher him- or herself.
6   Define priorities once the research is under way.
7   Serve as a guide for increasing the likelihood of successful completion on time.

The advantage of planning is that it:

1   Reduces the risk of overlooking something important.
2   Helps you to realise when you have run into difficulties.

3   Shows the relationship between your activities.

4   Orders your activities so that everything does not happen all at once.

5   Indicates whether your objectives are feasible in the time available. If not, something needs to change.

6   Provides discipline and motivation by indicating targets or milestones, and so is good for morale as you pass each milestone. It shows you are getting somewhere! Experience suggests that the best way to successful completion of the project as a whole is the successful completion of intermediate stages.

As I emphasised earlier, a further important aspect of such planning is that almost all research tasks have a writing component. The writing cannot be left until later in the first year, or the second or the third year. It is therefore important to add writing deadlines to your time planning.

The following is basic to the systematic organisation of your work.

1   List aims, objectives, research questions or hypotheses. (You have been working on this in the previous section.)

2   List what you need to do in order to achieve objectives, answer questions, etc. (You have done some work on this for the first three months of your project in Activity 3.1.)

3   Put the tasks in the order in which you will do them. Which comes before what? Which after? Which can be done concurrently?

4   Now put the tasks in sequence and estimate the time each one will need. (The next section looks in some detail at the important tasks of preparing a time budget and time schedule.)

5   Time the whole process and see whether what you have makes sense. Then do it all again as often as necessary.

ACTIVITY 3.5

Make a preliminary list of the tasks you think will be necessary in the first year of your project. Go on to sketch out the activities for the whole project.

The problem of time

At the start of a research project there seems to be so much time – how can the work expand to fill it? So why do students not finish on time? How can *you* finish on time?

This section offers some suggestions for preparing a *time budget* and a *time schedule*. We all tend to underestimate the time required for completing a research project. Hence a formal detailed estimating approach is likely to yield a better estimate than an overall estimate not using any breakdown. As indicated in the previous section, the first essential is to estimate the amount of time needed to complete each of your activities. Some typical activities for a questionnaire-based social science PhD are listed below, where Howard and Sharp (1989, p. 51) estimate durations in weeks. The total is a little over three years! Even so, it allows only nine weeks for drafts of the three early chapters, which are likely to include a significant literature (topic) review – see Chapter 5. Note that Howard and Sharp's list is more detailed than the generic list on p. 58, although it does not include the need to take relevant courses. It is used here as a guide to help you think about your work plan.

1   Written statement of concepts and theories: three weeks.
2   First draft of questionnaire for pilot study: six weeks.
3   Finalise questionnaire for pilot study: one week.
4   Decide likely method of analysing response to survey: four weeks.
5   Select participants for pilot study: four weeks.
6   Acquire statistical skills: eight weeks.
7   Attend course on use of standard computer package: six weeks.
8   Write drafts of early thesis chapters (three, say): nine weeks.
9   Carry out pilot study: four weeks.
10   Review pilot study: three weeks.
11   Prepare questionnaire for survey: four weeks.
12   Decide target population and sampling details: four weeks.
13   Carry out survey: twelve weeks.
14   Process data for computer: six weeks.
15   Interpret computer output: six weeks.
16   Evaluate nature and extent of response to survey: four weeks.
17   Write paper for presentation at conference: four weeks.
18   Relate findings to concepts/theories/hypotheses: six weeks.
19   Decide and carry out any further analysis or research: twelve weeks.
20   Complete writing of draft chapters (five, say): fifteen weeks.
21   Review and edit thesis: ten weeks.
22   Correct thesis and obtain bound copies: four weeks.
23   Prepare for oral examination: two weeks.
24   Allowance for holidays, job interviews, illness and general contingencies: twenty-four weeks.

The estimated *duration* referred to by Howard and Sharp is the *elapsed* time, that is, the time taken to complete an activity. This is usually longer than the number of hours/days of work entailed by the activity, because you may have difficulty contacting people or you may need more time to absorb and integrate new information into your project.

Time periods are difficult to estimate but will become more realistic with practice and experience. Your supervisor will advise, and you can also get valuable insights if you are able to discuss your plans with others who have already completed similar projects. Remember that it is necessary to allow for activities and occurrences that will not further your project work (for example, holidays or illness). Some activities will be carried out intermittently, some may be continually occupying your time and again presenting problems of estimation. This approach seems to assume that the initial topic proposal has been completed and that you are now at the stage of refining it. It is common to underestimate the weeks and months needed to document the research, often by several times. In fact, it is important to make estimates in the early stages of a research project, even when the middle and later stages cannot be tightly defined. Time is an important variable.

The next activity is designed to help you produce your own plan or schedule. It is important to attempt this activity. For a change, the example is a one-year research project of the BPhil type. That is why it is measured in hours, and is geared to a relatively tightly bounded project. You should change it to suit your needs. So, if you are doing an MPhil, you should produce a two-year schedule. If you are aiming for a PhD, do it for three years. If you are a part-time student it may be sensible to assume you will take twice as long. Therefore, allow four years for an MPhil and six years for a PhD. Instead of hours, you may prefer to use weeks, like Howard and Sharp. You will find it easier to think about the first year of the project but make estimates for the whole project.

The important idea is realistic planning and this depends on realistic time estimates. The best ones are usually made by breaking your activities down into smaller tasks and combining these estimates. Even if you have an activity that seems impossible to put a time on, you should still try to make an estimate. What you might do is to estimate the other activities and then include a pessimistic, an optimistic, and a best duration for the difficult-to-estimate activity. It is better to have a weak estimate than none at all.

ACTIVITY 3.6

Complete schedules 1–6 on the basis of your own project.

Schedule 1 Refining your proposal

Activity	Estimated duration (hours)
Preparation of revised proposal	....
Detailed outline of the final project report/thesis	....
Other	....
Total	....

Schedule 2 Search of the literature

| Sources to search | Estimated No. | Hours for each | | Actual duration (hours) |
		Standard estimate	Your estimate	
Journal articles	....	1.0	....	....
Books	....	10.0	....	....
Dissertations	....	5.0	....	....
Government documents	....	3.0	....	....
Other	....	....	....	....
Total				....

Schedule 3 Research activities

Activity	Estimated duration (hours)
Review of literature	....
Preparing means of collecting data (questionnaire, simulation, experiment, etc.)	....
Testing the instrument for collecting data	....
Collecting data (doing questionnaires, running experiments, etc.)	....
Data analysis	....
Applying concepts and theories	....
Analysis of results	....
Other	....
Total	....

Schedule 4 Writing, editing, rewriting

| Chapter/ section | Provisional title | Estimated No. of pages | Hours per page | | Actual duration (hours) |
			Standard estimate	Your estimate	
....	....	....	4	....	....
....	....	....	4	....	....
....	....	....	4	....	....
....	....	....	4	....	....
....	....	....	4	....	....
Summary/conclusion/recommendations		....	8	....	....
Appendices		....	....	....	....
Bibliography		....	6	....	....
Total		....			....

Schedule 5 Total estimated hours

Activity	Estimated hours
Revising and refining proposal	....
Literature search	....
Research activities	....
Writing, editing, rewriting	....
Total duration	....

Schedule 6 Estimated completion date

Activity	No. of days	Day	Month
Starting date of completion estimate		....	....
Working time (days)	....		
Estimated completion time (no delays)		....	....
Estimated completion time (no delays)			
Delays expected:			
Data collection	....		
Data analysis	....		
Chapter reading	....		
Final reading	....		
Typing and printing	....		
Other	....		
Estimated final completion data (ready for assessment)		....	....

After preparing your gross time budget, the activities need to be sequenced through time. Figure 3.2 shows a simple format for scheduling activities. You could also set up a list of critical review and target dates (for example, due dates for assignments to supervisor). One of the principles of doing this kind of schedule is that planned work will generally take precedence over unplanned work. The management task is to put enough structure into the planning process that it assumes a priority over other less important activities. Some people find it helpful to begin each week's project work with a planning hour and to establish specific tasks for the week, estimating times for each of the tasks. More tasks than can actually be completed might be outlined, putting priority on their execution. Those outlined that have a lower priority provide alternative tasks which can be started if the high-priority tasks cannot be completed for some reason. Finally, as tasks are completed the actual time taken could be recorded. Thus, at

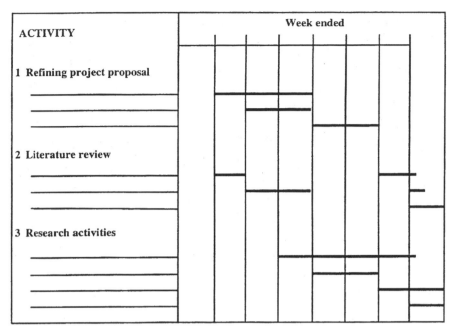

FIGURE 3.2
Schedule of
project
activities.
From OU
training pack
U500, *Doing
Academic
Research*

the planning session at the beginning of the next work week, the actual times can be compared with the estimated times and decisions can be made about the effectiveness of work and the amount of time that may need to be allocated for activities in the coming week.

Note that a schedule is a target. If you are not on target, your alternatives are:

1   Go faster.
2   Allocate more time at the expense of something else.
3   Scale down your objectives and hence the amount of activity needed.

The amount of detail that goes into planning is partly a matter of individual preference and temperament. Over-elaborate planning may be discouraging or time-wasting – planning charts in six colours, and so on – which can become procrastination to avoid starting the research. You *do* need some minimum amount of planning but do not frighten yourself or get bogged down by making it too elaborate (Bell, 1993; Howard and Sharp, 1989).

Discussion

A few issues regularly crop up as important in discussions with research students towards the end of their projects, when they reflect back on their research. Students often bring up these issues after a preliminary phrase like '... if only I'd done that in the first few months' or '... if only I'd stopped doing so much on that sooner'. The following is not a comprehensive list of tips, just a guide to a few of the more typical ones.

1   It is very easy to take too long over one task and try to do everything. For example, it is not possible to do a comprehensive literature review with every single relevant reference. The purpose of such a review is to build confidence that your project is relevant and that a 'gap' exists which your research will fill. It is not to gather every relevant reference.

2   The planning of a medium to long-term project, although absolutely key to success within the time available, cannot have perfect vision of everything that will be needed. It is good to be flexible and to be prepared to add and subtract tasks from time to time, after suitable discussion with supervisors.

3   Do be prepared to add tasks that no one has suggested. You are a good judge of key tasks. For example, I had excellent supervision for my PhD but no one ever suggested the importance of meeting key researchers near the start of a research project. Students are often surprised that senior researchers are pleased to be asked about their research by people just beginning. They can turn out to be extremely supportive, useful contacts at conferences and formal events. Even potential external examiners can be approached. Talk to them early.

4   Last, but not least, something will go wrong in every research project. When it does, the first instinct is usually to panic or freeze. It is important at that moment to remind yourself, however anxious you are, that such events happen to everyone. You should write down the problem as carefully as you can, since writing something down can often help sort out more clearly what the issues are that need to be resolved. But it is at times like these that supervisors are important. The issues usually need to be discussed as soon as possible so that alternatives can be found, or ways round the problem navigated.

Setting a milestone

I began the previous section by suggesting that the beginning of a research project opens a panorama of limitless time. As the first few months go by the long lists of possible tasks often create a sobering and sometimes frightening chaos. Time planning, such as that suggested in the preceding section, is a way of helping with the task of prioritising work. Is today's task in your plan? If not, is it important enough to be there? If it is not that important, why are you doing it? These are questions that may guide you as you spend your first months organising your research project.

At the beginning of this chaper I said that, by the end of it you should feel reasonably confident about the milestones you have set yourself in the first year. On p. 60 I mentioned that one well known problem in doing a research project is how to manage time. Many of us cannot work to 'theoretical' deadlines – we need them to be written down and carefully monitored. Others stay with the 'easy' tasks, avoiding those that require hard thought or focus. Yet others focus on the hardest tasks, making little progress and not doing any of the easier tasks either! The previous section is an attempt to help you plan and prioritise your work.

I often say, 'I must finish this by the end of the week.' But, if I have not made a promise to deliver, or been told to deliver, the chances of it happening on time are not very great. So it is with research milestones. Your supervisor(s) will, doubtless, ask you to deliver pieces of work. But you are the key person in formulating sensible milestones. Milestones can be daily, weekly, monthly or longer. Your research journal is the obvious place to set yourself deadlines. I always recommend weekly and monthly stocktaking. It need take no longer than an hour.

But there are bigger milestones in the first year of a two- or three-year project. As you already know from your work so far in this chapter, they may include:

1   Getting a laboratory experiment up and running.
2   Trying out your thesis ideas and plan on your supervisor(s) and other students.
3   Drafting a literature survey/topic review.

Each major task actually constitutes a serious milestone. Each one can be written up, and can often be used as early drafts of your thesis.

ACTIVITY 3.7

The remainder of the chapter concentrates on getting you to think about preparing a short presentation (twenty minutes) that would be suitable to put to your supervisor(s) as part of your first-year evaluation process.
The previous activities in this chapter, taken together, will make this activity easy. A twenty-minute presentation is relatively short, so you will have to think hard about the key points you want to make in order to give your supervisor a clear idea of your progress and future plans. You may decide to include the following, but it is just a guide: your research question(s) or hypotheses; a plan of how you will do the research in the first year; and the issues that need addressing with your supervisor(s).
Make notes on a structure for your presentation, using the materials you already have on:

1 Your research idea.
2 Your research questions/hypotheses/aims.
3 Why the research is important.
4 What are the key research tasks in the first year.
5 How you might set about these tasks.
6 Making a research plan for the first year, and sketching a plan for the whole project, with time scales.
7 What may be the key issues on which you want advice from your supervisor(s).

Most research students in their first year have (at least) two such milestones. One is to produce a 'literature review' or 'topic review' for their project. This is the subject of Chapter 5. The second milestone is to produce a detailed work plan. If your project is for one year, you will do this in the first few months. For a two- or three-year project the detailed work plan will usually be produced at the six- to nine-month point.

Discussion and conclusion

Ask your supervisor(s) to give you feedback on Activity 3.7. Your work on this activity will probably fit the bill for at least a part of your first-year assessment. To finish, I have included examples of a full-time student's work done at the sixth-month point of a doctoral programme (the equivalent of month 12 for a part-timer). The following comes from Terry Newholm, who was mentioned earlier (see Box 3.5). He was trying to translate his research question into a series of empirical data collection tasks.

Research question: Why do most consumers report holding stronger (and wider) ethical views than their purchasing patterns would suggest?

Empirical work: how do I go about it?

5   Methodology
5.1   Locating respondents/co-researchers:
1   *How do I find an ordinary bunch of 'ethical' consumers to work with?*
2   In view of many people's enthusiasm to discuss the issue, and my personal involvement, would it be better to think of respondents as co-researchers?
3   Are they case studies because they cannot be representative?
5.2   Prior to research:
1   *Would it be a good idea to ask respondents/co-researchers to keep a log of purchases for a month/week as an aid to memory?*
2   Do I try to categorise respondents/co-researchers into strong and weak ethicals like the market researchers or in some relevant social categories? (There is ample evidence that women and men see ethical consumer issues differently.)
3   Would it help to, and how would I, be able to assess the respondents/co-researchers' aims in life to see how relatively important a component ethics is, or could I just assess their total consumption?
4   Are there standard (psychological) ways of assessing what people see as their approach to life, i.e. pleasure seeking, security seeking, etc.?
5.3   Unstructured/semi-structured interviews:
1   Should interviews be unstructured or semi-structured?
2   *How do I assess whether respondents/co-researchers have both ethical and hedonistic consumer desires and if there is conflict between them?*

3   If I believe that consumers may try to avoid personal ethical responsibility for issues how should I get 'below' this level of explanation?

4   Should I ask respondents/co-researchers if they can identify 'role models' or a 'path' for their consumption in general and as ethical consumers?

5   How can I reduce the chances of respondents/co-researchers 'telling me what I want to hear'?

5.4 Group meetings:

1   *Should I try to return any findings to a group discussion, with respondents because peer group effects might be important constituents of the process?*

5.5 Results:

1   How do I discuss/evaluate the findings?

2   *How could I assess the narratives respondents/co-researchers tell?*

3   Will I finally be asking can any of the theories be supported by the research findings?

4   What other sources of evidence/research can I find to support (triangulate) my results?

References

Bell, J. (1993) *Doing Your Research Project*, Milton Keynes, Open University Press.

Buchanan, D. (1980) 'Gaining management skills through academic research work', *Personnel Management*, April.

Dey, I. (1993) *Qualitative Data Analysis*, London, Routledge.

Howard, K. and Sharp, J. A. (1989) *The Management of a Student Research Project*, Aldershot, Gower.

Morse, J. M. (1994) 'Designing funded qualitative research', in N. K. Denzin and Y. S. Lincoln, (eds) *Handbook of Qualitative Research*, pp. 220–35, London, Sage.

Murdick, G. and Cooper, D. (1982) *Business Research: Concepts and Guides*, Columbus OH, Grid.

Murray, R. (1996) *Thesis Writing*, University of Strathclyde, Centre for Academic Practice.

Phillips, E. M. and Pugh, D. S. (1987) *How to Get a PhD*, Milton Keynes, Open University Press.

Smith, P. A. (1988) 'Quality of Nursing and the Ward as a Learning Environment for Student Nurses: a multi-method approach', PhD thesis, London University.

Stone, E. (1987) *Research Methods in Organizational Behavior*, Santa Monica CA, Goodyear.

Tagg, C. (1996) *Exploring the Qualitative Quagmire for Information Systems Research*, UKAIS Conference, Cranfield, 10–12 April.

Verma, G. K. and Beard, R. M. (1981) *What is Educational Research? Perspectives on Techniques of Research*, Aldershot, Gower.

Wright Mills, C. (1978) *The Sociological Imagination*, Harmondsworth, Penguin.

Acknowledgements

Grateful acknowledgement is made to Gower Publishing Ltd, Aldershot, for permission to reproduce the list of activities on pp. 62–64, from K. Howard and J. A. Sharp, *The Management of a Student Research Project*, second edition (1996).

Chapter 4

The Writing Process

Andrew Ward

After reading this chapter you will be able to:

- **Get into the writing habit**

- **Create the right conditions**

- **Get yourself started**

- **Structure your draft and draw up a synopsis**

- **Put flesh on the skeleton**

- **Set yourself targets**

- **Get feedback on your work**

- **Overcome writer's block**

- **Rewrite and edit**

- **Avoid the usual pitfalls of academic writing**

> No research has been done, in any sense that counts, until the writing has
> been done, and those who speak of 'writing up' rather than writing betray
> a total ignorance of what they are at.
>
> (Watson, 1987, p. 40)

It is no longer fashionable to talk of 'writing up' as if it were a separate stage that
follows the research. It is also outdated to view writing skills as synonymous
with correct grammar (as teachers did in the 1950s) or good handwriting (as in
the 1920s). Nowadays it is common to talk of the *writing process*.

The writing process is the elaborate means by which idle thoughts are converted into coherent, readable text.

> Just as the research process is not a neat, clean progression from one step
> to another, so the writing process tends to be recursive. Some sections of
> your paper may fall into place in the second draft. Other sections may be
> more stubborn; you may have to revise five or six times as you work to find
> out how the parts fit together. As you write, you may decide that the thesis
> you are developing is not the thesis you started with.
>
> (Hubbuch, 1989, p. 119)

This chapter, therefore, is designed to raise your awareness of the various hidden
activities which combine to form the process of writing a thesis – planning,
structuring, drafting text, reading text, negotiating feedback, rewriting and editing. By the end of the chapter you will, ideally, have learned some techniques to
improve your writing and you will have become more professional in your
approach. This is important because the writing process is common to all writers, whether they be professionals who write every day or thesis writers. The content of their work, their writing style and level of argument may vary
significantly, of course, but the process of getting there is the same.

> Professional writers do not do anything different from occasional or casual
> writers, though they may do it more efficiently and more effectively. They
> may know what the occasional writer strives to know.
>
> (Smith, 1982, pp. v–vi)

The writing process is all-encompassing. Your writing should interact with your
reading, your reasoning and your research. Recognition of this frees you to establish good writing *habits* from the moment you begin your research degree (see
the next section).

There is a case for this chapter being the first in the book. After all, your
ultimate goal is a *written* thesis and your work should be directed towards that
goal. If you grow too accustomed to labels such as 'research student', 'postgraduate student' or 'researcher' you may lose sight of your essential role as *writer*.
One student said:

This sounds a bit odd, but I never got the impression that writing up the thesis was the primary objective of doing my PhD. I got the impression that the idea was to do experiments and get the results out in presentations and papers, and the thesis would happen by itself. The thesis wasn't my focus. Nowadays, as a professional writer rather than as a scientist, my whole focus is on what I'm writing. Now, when I get a writing brief, I immediately think about how the final piece is going to look.

This chapter's major purpose is to provoke you into thinking of yourself as a writer. As Smith (1982) has said, 'Writing is learned by writing, reading and *perceiving oneself as a writer*' (my italics). Only by writing can you improve your confidence as a writer. Only by viewing yourself as a writer can you become aware of the writing skills that you need to develop. And only by aspiring to become more professional can you improve your skills.

Much of your writing will be done in isolation. Some writers argue that feeling comfortable about yourself in a solitary setting is the most important thing about writing well. This raises a lot of questions about your writing environment and what (and whom) you need around you (see pp. 79–83). Others argue that the most important thing is to find tricks to get your writing started on the days when you want to write (see pp. 83–84).

If this is your first work of dissertation length, you may need to learn how to structure and organise a large piece of work (see pp. 84–92) and set targets so that you can break your work down into more familiar short-term goals (see pp. 92–94). These skills should be developed as soon as possible. One researcher found that many postgraduate failures were 'better at putting things into box files than getting them out' (Rudd, 1985).

When writing at length, you will become more emotionally involved with your work and therefore feedback needs sensitive negotiation and careful consideration (see pp. 94–96). Motivation has to be maintained over a long period and there is more chance of getting stuck and running into difficulties. However, writers find all sorts of ways of writing themselves out of trouble and sustaining progress (see pp. 96–100).

You will also need to revise and edit your work. Early drafts tend to be writer-oriented (what you are trying to say) and later drafts will be more reader-conscious (what makes sense to the reader) (see pp. 100–106).

In the past, education systems have hindered the development of thesis-writing skills. Examinations encouraged small, one-off writing projects with no feedback, no revision, no editing, no long-term planning and no opportunity for writers to choose their favoured environment (Smith, 1982, p. 204). The school system can also perpetuate the myth that writing is boring (Rudestam and Newton, 1992). Moreover, students are limited in the number of writers they can observe as role models; writing usually takes place behind closed doors and early drafts are hidden from the public. I would not dare show you some of the embarrassing starts I made to this chapter.

It is assumed that you have some writing experience. You would not have reached this stage in your career without some writing talent. But is your talent suited to a thesis? Will you need to learn new skills? And do you still have the writing habit?

Good habits

> Studies of academic writers ... show that brief, daily regimens produce more (and better) writing than does the popular practice of bingeing.
>
> (Griffiths, 1994, p. 460)

Professional writers offer one piece of advice above all others – make writing a daily habit. The importance of writing all the way through your research cannot be overstressed. The best place to start is in a notebook or journal.

> Your researcher's notebook is probably the most important item in your research project. It is a journal of what is happening in your *head* as you examine your evidence.
>
> (Hubbuch, 1989, p. 13)

The importance of a research journal has already been mentioned in earlier chapters, and it should capture your reading and research in such a way that you can create an early first draft. Here again, though, you should try as hard as possible to identify yourself as a *writer* (rather than as a note taker). This is because the skills of writing and note taking are different, and some students get stuck in the note-taking role (Nelson, 1993, p. 91). Try to use your notebook both for the mechanical act of taking notes *and* for the creative act of composing writing. It is also important to convert your notes into something akin to writing while your research is fresh and your enthusiasm strong.

This may help you to acquire the daily act of writing. Good prose cannot be turned on like water from a tap. Writers, like marathon runners, reach their peak when they are in practice. As Dorothea Brande advises, in her classic book *Becoming a Writer*, write something (anything) every day. One way to start is to get up half an hour earlier than usual:

> Write anything that comes into your head: last night's dream, if you are able to remember it; the activities of the day before; a conversation, real or imaginary; an examination of conscience. Write any sort of early morning reverie, rapidly and uncritically. The excellence or ultimate worth of what you write is of no importance yet. As a matter of fact, you will find more value in this material than you expect, but your primary purpose now is not to bring forth deathless words, but to write any words at all which are not pure nonsense.
>
> (Brande, 1996, p. 66)

Some academic departments encourage the writing habit by demanding that students write up specific parts of the thesis, in draft, as part of the year's schedule.

For example, students who have proposed their research method are asked to draft their research-method chapter. This gives a powerful sense of writing being accomplished along the way. As Rudd (1985, p. 130) says, 'Seeing written work is the best way to judge progress, as there is less scope for fluffing in the written than in the spoken word'. One student said:

> My PhD was in biochemistry, and I was actually a few steps ahead of the people I worked alongside because I had done monthly reports for my supervisor. He encouraged me to submit reports on the first of each month, and in those reports I had all the experimental methods I had used over the three years, plus references and results. I also had lab notebooks of what I was doing. Losing those would have been a disaster.

There are other ways to establish a regular writing regime. As soon as you have finished studying a discrete block of material, write a summary to test your understanding. Or write down your research questions on a regular basis, thus documenting how you see them changing as you read more about the subject. Alternatively, write about what is important to you about your thesis, or about any problems you are having – anything to get the habit going.

> A lot of times you don't feel like writing and you just have to stick it out. Sometimes I start work not remotely in the mood but after about an hour it starts getting okay. As an adolescent one was mood-driven. You can't be mood-driven as an adult.

Another useful technique to generate writing is to tape-record any regular conversations with your supervisor or colleagues. Then transcribe the tapes afterwards and write up anything that you may use in your final thesis. The process of writing will help clear the mind and highlight gaps in your thinking and problems that have not been faced (Rudd, 1985). The development of writing skill can therefore contribute to higher-level reasoning skills and better subject understanding (Applebee, 1984).

The basic aim is an early draft of your thesis, no matter how rough-and-ready it may be, no matter how many gaps there are.

The research proposal

Madsen (1983, p. 35) viewed the research proposal as the key element in a successful dissertation. He suggested the following format.

1   Cover page (proposed title, author, address, telephone number, institution, degree sought, names of advisory members, date of submission).
2   One-page abstract (approximately 350 words). The final abstract, a summary of the thesis, will appear around the world, enabling other scholars to gain an understanding of what you have achieved. It should contain concise answers to all the key questions outlined by Madsen (1983, p. 82):

(a) What is your research question?
(b) Why is it important?
(c) What theoretical framework was used in the research?
(d) What data were collected?
(e) How were the data analysed?
(f) What special techniques (if any) were used?
(g) What were your results?

Obviously, it is not possible to answer all these questions at the proposal stage, but you can experiment to see how your final abstract may look.

3   Statement of the research problem (four to fourteen pages):

(a) Introduction.
(b) Research question (interrogative sentence, definition of terms).
(c) Subsidiary questions (hypotheses).
(d) Review of relevant research and theory (integrated with respect to your key questions).

4   Procedure (four to fourteen pages):

(a) Description of the theoretical or conceptual framework to be used.
(b) Sources of evidence and authority.
(c) Analytical technique and research design.
(d) Timetable for completing the thesis.

5   A trial table of contents (one to two pages).
6   Brief bibliography (one to five pages).

It may help to discuss the results of this activity in a pair or a group. You can also 'brainstorm' creative ways to improve, or sustain, your writing habit. Four examples are: (1) start a newsletter and write reports of conferences and research findings; (2) try to find a place where you can write a regular column; (3) give pieces of writing to friends and relatives as birthday or Christmas presents (for example, collections of anecdotes); or (4) invent collaborative writing games for fun (see p. 78).

Return to this activity periodically to check how your habit is progressing. You may also wish to find a supportive writing buddy (or establish a writing group) with whom you can meet regularly to focus on writing issues. It need not be someone from your own discipline – it could be anybody who is interested in writing. Rowena Murray (1997) has successfully organised writers' support groups within academic settings. They meet for one to two hours a week for six months.

Strategies for improving writing productivity

Griffiths (1994) lists fourteen strategies for improving writing productivity. He stresses that not every suggestion will work for everyone.

ACTIVITY 4.1

Professional writers measure productivity by number of words written rather than hours or minutes spent on writing. On Schedule 1 estimate the number of words you write during the current week (while at work or at leisure). Include any type of writing and add more sections if necessary. Try to complete the grid for each day as it happens.

Schedule 1 Number of words written in a week

Type of writing	Sunday	Monday	Tuesday	Wednesday	Thursday	Friday	Saturday
Letters	....	....	....	....	....	....	....
Minutes of meetings	....	....	....	....	....	....	....
With supervisor	....	....	....	....	....	....	....
With students	....	....	....	....	....	....	....
Diary	....	....	....	....	....	....	....
Journal	....	....	....	....	....	....	....
Research notebook	....	....	....	....	....	....	....
Poems	....	....	....	....	....	....	....
Short stories	....	....	....	....	....	....	....
Therapeutic writing	....	....	....	....	....	....	....
E-mails	....	....	....	....	....	....	....
Articles	....	....	....	....	....	....	....
Academic papers	....	....	....	....	....	....	....
Reports	....	....	....	....	....	....	....
Witness statements	....	....	....	....	....	....	....
Thesis chapter	....	....	....	....	....	....	....
Other	....	....	....	....	....	....	....

When the grid is complete, try to reflect on some key questions:

1 Did you write every day?
2 Did you average between 500 and 1,000 words a day?
3 Was your writing output fairly even?
4 Which pieces did you rewrite and edit? (Encircle any entries that went through more than one draft.)
5 In what ways can you improve your writing habit?

1   Establish one (or a few) regular place(s) where *all* serious writing is done.
2   Remove all temptations and distractions from the writing site (for example, magazines and television).
3   Leave other activities (for example, washing up and cooking dinner) until after writing.
4   Limit potential interruptions (for example, put a 'Do not disturb' sign on the door, unplug the telephone).
5   Find another writer to share writing space for mutual quiet periods of work.
6   Make the writing site as comfortable as possible.
7   Make regular recurrent activity (for example, telephone calls, coffee making) dependent on minimum periods of writing first.
8   Write while feeling 'fresh' and leave mentally untaxing activities until later in the day.
9   Plan beyond daily goals and be realistic about what can be written in the time available.
10   Schedule writing tasks into manageable units (i.e. make rough plans).
11   Complete one section of writing at a time if the writing is in sections.
12   Use a word processor (if possible) to make drafting easier.
13   Revise and redraft at least twice.
14   Share writing with a supportive, constructive colleague, as people are more helpful, judgemental and critical about 'unfinished' drafts.

Example of a co-operative group writing game

Each player has a blank sheet of paper and a pen. Each player chews the end of the pen while thinking what to write. Each player writes the last line (line 10) of a (very) short story. The paper is folded and put in the centre of the table. Each player picks out a sheet to write the first line (line 1) of the same (very) short story. It is advisable for the first line to be as far removed, conceptually or geographically, from the last as possible, as it will cause anguish among the other players. Something catastrophic at line 8 has the same effect. Players pick sheets at random for each round until they have written 10 lines between them, linking line 1 with line ten (more or less). Players are not allowed to write two successive lines. Then you draw one at random, give it a title and read it out (when it's your turn). Criticism is banned. Only praise and laughter are allowed. (Source: adapted from *The Oxford Writer*, July 1997.)

Example of a competitive group writing game

Each player finds an academic paper that may be of interest to all members of the group. It could concern your subject, or study skills, or it could be something quirky and topical. It is better if the rest of the group are not acquainted with your papers. When it is your turn, you introduce the paper by referring briefly to its methodology. Then, on a small piece of paper, each member of the group writes what they think would be a suitable first line for the paper. Meanwhile you write the real first line on a piece of paper. You collect together all the first lines and give each one a separate number. Then you read them aloud, trying to keep a straight face (not always easy). You usually have to do this twice. Each person (except you) votes for the one they think is the real first line written by the *bona fide* published academic. (Each player votes by holding up a small piece of paper with a number on.) A player wins a point by guessing correctly, and also wins a point if somebody falls for the line they wrote. (For later rounds you can shift to the first line of different sections of the same paper, or you can read out a passage and ask people to write the last line.)

A writer's environment

> For all the mystery that surrounds it, *feng shui* evolved from the simple observation that people are affected, for good or ill, by surroundings: the layout and orientation of workplaces and homes.
>
> (Rossbach, 1991, p. 2)

Barbara Cartland has dictated novels from a sofa, a white fur rug over her legs, a hot water bottle at her feet, two dogs beside her and a secretary with shorthand notebook at the ready. Robert Graves and Ernest Hemingway wrote while standing up. Truman Capote's favoured position was lying on a bed with a typewriter on his knees. Nick Virgilio, an American poet, sometimes writes while standing on his head because he believes he has 15 per cent more brain power when blood is rushing to the brain. What works for you?

Dunn *et al.* (1992, pp. 17–18) have shown differences in learning styles for people studying difficult information. Analytical learners require a quiet environment with a bright light, a hard chair and a desk, and they work away at a single task until they reach a meal-break or complete the task. In contrast, global learners enjoy the sound of chatter or music, a soft light and an informal setting such as a settee, and they work on several tasks while chewing, eating, drinking or smoking.

The secret is to create a work environment suitable for getting *your work* done. You may find that certain conditions are a requirement to your effectiveness, while others are optional. Successful writers certainly know how to get the best out of themselves. One good source for picturing writers in their natural habitat is the *Paris Review* 'Writers at Work' series (Cowley, 1982; Plimpton, 1982–8), a collection of seven books containing interviews with famous writers. After discovering the vagaries of writers, and the variation in learning styles, you are free to develop an idiosyncrasy or two. But do you know what your best way of working is? What may you need in order to maximise your writing output? Are there conditions that you simply have to put up with? 'I often fantasise about having my own study where no-one could invade my space,' said one PhD student. 'Sadly, this is not always possible.' Writers who agree with this student often believe that attitude towards work is more important than the setting. What matters is your ability to concentrate on work whatever the setting and construct a 'wall of silence' (Murray, 1984, p. 43) or an 'artistic coma' (Brande, 1996).

Alternatively, there are writers who believe that you can be more productive if you create the best possible conditions for yourself. Consider the following professional writer.

If I was writing a PhD now and fitting it in around a day job, I would control my work space and make it a different environment from my day-job surroundings and different again from where I spend my leisure time. I would create a good atmosphere so that I wanted to be in the place and I wanted to write when I was there. And I would want it to be my space. I wouldn't want to waste time putting things away and taking them out. You have to treat the demanding task of writing a thesis with the seriousness it deserves. I don't think it is coincidence that the two most successful and productive writers I know have purpose-built outhouses where they can work while protected from the quicksand of daily living.

There is probably some truth in both these theories – you need good concentration for all surroundings and yet you need to create favourable conditions for your regular work space. Here are the views of an experienced study-skills counsellor:

Younger students come to college with parental strictures ringing in their ears – you can't work with that music on, how can you lie on your bed and write, etc. – and it's almost through a process of maturity that they realise that they do need to organise their work area. When students are sent to me because they are not 'getting it together', I always start by asking them, 'Where do you live? Where do you work? How do you go about the process of getting down to work?' Nearly always they turn out not to have a system. I spent one support seminar discussing good places to work – spotting the quiet rooms or the little-used library spaces. The feedback from those who tried the collective suggestions was a kind of 'Wow, I didn't realise it made so much difference.'

When I lead this activity on training courses, discussion generally focuses on three key issues: (1) dealing with interruptions; (2) the advantages and disadvantages of using computers, in particular the specific disadvantages of repetitive strain injury; and (3) the reasons for designing your work space.

Dealing with interruptions

Writers need a discipline that minimises interruptions. Some techniques of doing this are fairly obvious – an answerphone with the volume turned down, 'Do not disturb' signs and not answering the door – but others may need the careful work of negotiation with a partner, children, or work colleagues.

Successful professional writers often rent an office, but most of us have to find ways of making do with our own environment. There are several cheap options, such as exchanging space with a neighbour, or working in a friend's house while they are away. One writer found it difficult to explain to his children that he could not play with them even though he was in the house. He overcame the problem by waving them goodbye at the front door, walking down the street, round the back of the house, in the back door, and stealthily slipping upstairs to his study.

ACTIVITY 4.2

What is your preferred environment for writing? What works best for *you*?
Tick the boxes that apply.

1 How do you prefer to write?
  ☐ Sitting down
  ☐ Lying down
  ☐ Standing up
  ☐ Standing on your head
2 What equipment do you prefer?
  ☐ Ballpoint pen
  ☐ Pencil
  ☐ Manual typewriter
  ☐ Personal computer
  ☐ Fancy fountain pen
  ☐ Lap top computer
  ☐ Tape recorder
3 What other stationery do you need?
  ☐ Paper clips
  ☐ Special paper
  ☐ Stapler
  ☐ Ruler
  ☐ Eraser
  ☐ Tipp-Ex
  ☐ Other ...
4 Which books do you like to keep
  nearby?
  ☐ Dictionary
  ☐ Fowler's *Modern English Usage*
  ☐ Thesaurus
  ☐ *Dictionary for Writers and Editors*
  ☐ *Copy-Editing* (Butcher)
  ☐ Other ...
5 Where do you prefer to work?
  ☐ At home
  ☐ In an open-plan office
  ☐ In a private office
  ☐ In a library
  ☐ In a pub
  ☐ In a café
  ☐ On a train
  ☐ Other ...

6 When do you work best?
  ☐ Morning
  ☐ Afternoon
  ☐ Evening
  ☐ Late at night
7 When do you reach top form?
  ☐ During the first 10 minutes
  ☐ During the first hour
  ☐ During the second hour
  ☐ After several hours
8 What other conditions do you
  prefer?
  ☐ Natural light from a window
  ☐ Overhead light/desk-light
  ☐ A view
  ☐ No view
  ☐ Space to pace around
  ☐ Clutter
  ☐ Quiet
  ☐ Background noise
  ☐ Other ...
9 What interruptions do you permit?
  ☐ Telephone
  ☐ Friends
  ☐ Children
  ☐ Students
  ☐ Secretaries
  ☐ Other ...
10 Where do you get your best ideas?
  ☐ Lying in the bath
  ☐ Driving the car
  ☐ On a train or bus
  ☐ When reading
  ☐ In conversation
  ☐ When awake at night
  ☐ Walking the dog
  ☐ When writing
  ☐ Other ...

If you cannot totally control your environment, which are the most important of these factors to try to control?

The advantages and disadvantages of using a computer

The major problem caused by using computers is repetitive strain injury (RSI). As this is discussed at length elsewhere (see Chapter 6, 'Using computers in research'), my role here is simply to stress the value of reading that chapter. It is important to do sensible exercises and to heed the words of Booth (1985, p. 25): 'For the good of your health I strongly recommend that you alternate between sitting and standing.'

More positively, computers help in many ways (see Chapter 6 again). Word-processing packages allow us to edit without having to retype. We can change the structure of a piece more easily by moving blocks of text. We can experiment. Such is the power of computer packages that all professional writers should be aware of what they can achieve for them. Rudestam and Newton (1992) devote chapter 10 of their book *Surviving Your Dissertation* to using a personal computer effectively. Hammond (1984) was the first to devote a whole book to the subject. For a time the Society of Authors published a magazine called *The Electronic Author* but it has since been subsumed in the society's main magazine, *The Author*, because electronic issues are now considered relevant to all authors.

However, computers do not do it all for you. They are only a part of a writer's repertoire. While there are packages for checking spelling and grammar, they can be cumbersome and are far from foolproof. I have also heard professional writers argue that computers do not make you a better writer. The reasons they give are:

1   They tie you too much to one place. ('I can't write without my computer but now I've bought a laptop.')
2   They do not enable you to see the whole work. ('I have to print it out before I can edit it.')
3   They encourage you to be more casual. ('I don't think through my sentences and paragraphs like I did when I worked with a typewriter because now I know I can change them.')
4   They encourage writers to change text too quickly. ('I wish I'd saved the original sentence; I think it was probably better.')
5   They make writers more anxious about their writing. ('I feel it has to be right first time.')
6   They stifle creativity and lead to a different kind of writer's block. ('I hate staring at a blank screen.')
7   They make everything look so good that you are seduced into thinking that the writing is good ('I can write rubbish but it's beautifully laid out').

However, all these arguments are susceptible to counter-arguments. If you are aware of the issues, and you are constantly assessing your writing ability, then computers are a great asset. But remember to create back-up files. One writer I know creates floppy-disk back-ups every day. I try to keep a copy of work in progress at a friend's house, just in case. They also say that you should keep your manuscript in the freezer – it is usually the last place to burn in a house fire – but make sure you use a waterproof bag in case the ice melts.

Designing your work space

Feng shui consultants will tell you that environments can be made more productive. They believe that mysterious earth forces are responsible for determining health, prosperity and good luck, and we should respect these earth forces when designing work spaces, finding ways to nourish the residents' *ch'i* (human energy). An ill-designed interior is asking for trouble – stress, irritability and, ultimately, unhappiness.

I had been sceptical about ways of improving my environment, but I read books on *feng shui*, followed suggestions for changing my office space, and suddenly my work energy was buzzing. I moved my desk into the corner opposite the door and sat so that I could see the door. I put plants and bright lights in the suggested positions and placed a crystal alongside my computer. Well, it worked for me.

The books I read on *feng shui* were by Rossbach (1987, 1991), Spear (1995) and Kingston (1996), but plenty of other people have documented the principles of this ancient Chinese art. Many people, however, have a natural feel for what creates good work energy.

Conclusion

Ultimately, you must find ways to feel comfortable about being alone when you are writing a thesis. This may mean optimising environmental conditions to suit your effectiveness, or it may mean not being fazed by things beyond your control. As Smith (1982, p. 133) succinctly puts it, 'We should learn to trust our own best way of writing.'

Getting started

> For me, and most other writers I know, writing is not rapturous. In fact the only way I can get anything written at all is to write really, really shitty first drafts.
>
> (Lamott, 1995, p. 22)

Authors, like athletes, need to warm up. Whereas sprinters stretch their muscles and focus their minds on the forthcoming race, writers have their own individual ways of preparing for the task ahead:

> It takes Beryl Bainbridge about four months to write a novel. During this period she begins work at ten each evening and works through until four or five in the morning … Before starting to write in the evening she has to tidy the house: she will wash the dishes, or decide the stairs need cleaning

or the hedge needs cutting. She can only work in a perfectly ordered environment.

(Seymour-Smith, 1980, p. 86)

The trick is to understand what is legitimate warm-up and what is a distraction. The way to measure this is by assessing whether you have achieved your writing target for the day. There is no single right way of warming up. There is only one definite wrong way – when you do not achieve your writing target.

The best way to warm up is by writing, while telling yourself that your writing will get better as the day progresses. Journalists are taught the value of this when writing an article. They know that their most important paragraph is the first one, which is designed to hook the reader and summarise the article's importance. They also know that it will sometimes be the last paragraph they write, when they are warmed up and clear about what they are writing.

Goldberg (1991) provides several warm-up prompts: for example, write something that begins with 'I remember' or 'I want to write about'. For your thesis, you may wish to develop your own favourite prompts: 'Somewhere in my thesis I need to say something about ...'

ACTIVITY 4.3

Read Appendix 4.1, 'Twenty-six ways to start writing' from *Write to Learn* by Donald Murray (1984), at the end of this chapter. Make a list of what you think are the ten best ideas for helping you. Rank these ideas, write them on a postcard and pin it up near your work space. Add to them from other sources. (Note that Murray's book is called *Write to Learn* and not *Learn to Write*. He believes that it is only through the process of writing that you learn what you really want to say.)

There may be some days when even Murray's tips do not get you started. Then the problem may be more deep-seated. This issue, often referred to as 'writer's block', is considered in more detail in the last section of this chapter (p. 96).

Structure

Until I find it [the right structure] I am lost. I must be able to identify the end product as a total work in which every item has its proper and subordinate place ... [and] if I have not identified this appropriate structure, I waste my time if I try to write, for I will produce nothing.

(James Michener, quoted by Hayes, 1984, p. 217)

Authors who work on a large canvas will often tell you that the single most important thing that gives them the momentum to move forward is the idea for a structure, that is, how the parts will join together to form the whole. If you have a structure in mind from early in the project it will help you decide which information is relevant and which is not, and it will help you file your data.

A more detailed synopsis will enable you to estimate the number of words in each section of your thesis, so that you can break it down into manageable chunks (see p. 92 on setting targets). It will then free you to start the writing from any point. You do not have to write the thesis in the order in which it will appear.

Your draft structure must be flexible – expert writers are more willing to change the structure than novice writers – but it should be good enough to get you through the early stages. For example, one writer says about structure:

> *Right from the start of my writing career, back in the mid-seventies, my basic approach has been to plan carefully and then try to write quite fast. The first stage of my planning is to note a quick and instinctive overarching structure of the book in broad terms. This is back-of-an-envelope stuff but absolutely crucial. Within this structure a lot may happen, but somehow it can all be held together if this larger structure is in place. If it's a huge book I have different parts to the book, so that the chapters fit within the parts. I may make some later decisions about chapters but I certainly have the parts worked out. My thesis was structured around five substantial chapters. Each chapter had an overarching theme – a bit like a pack of cards which could be shuffled as to which order I played them in. For almost the entire length of the thesis, the chapter on 'new issues on the stock exchange' was going to be my last chapter, and it was definitely the most difficult chapter to write. Then someone suggested putting this chapter in the middle rather than at the end. Why not end with a very strong chapter? And that's what I did. It sounds very simple but I remember that it was a great relief at the time.*

A structure to live with

The structure you choose will always be flawed. The intellect required for a PhD thesis is multidimensional, whereas the structure of your thesis is unidimensional and linear. Novelists experiment with all sorts of structures to overcome this basic flaw, including ones where you can dip into a book at any place. Most of us, however, have to accept that we must choose one functional structure from the many possible ones.

Becker (1986) deals with this problem very well, using his own thesis as an example. His doctoral research involved the study of social relations in schools. He found that important relationships, say between teachers and parents, differed from one type of school to another. At first, Becker could not decide whether to offer his readers a background discussion of the types of school first and then present his findings about relationships or, alternatively, to discuss his major findings on relationships first and then look at differences in types of school. Becker's conclusion was that there was no one right way. Writers have to choose a way that works for them, a structure they can justify, and then get on with it. There is no use worrying about it. This is what Becker chose:

1   Teacher relations, with:

   (a) Pupils.
   (b) Parents.
   (c) Principals.
   (d) Other teachers.

2   Schools

   (a) Slum schools.
   (b) Working-class schools.
   (c) Upper- and middle-class schools.

If Becker had put the schools section before teacher relations it would have affected the outcome only in the way he would refer to other sections within the thesis, and terms such as 'as will be discussed in section 2' would be replaced by 'as was discussed in section 1'. That's all. And the same argument applies to literature/topic reviews.

It is very rare for a thesis to be failed on the basis of bad structure. The only reason for it to happen would be if the structure were unsuited to the content. However, people may fail if they do not come up with a structure early enough and are therefore hindered in their progress.

Alternative structures

Howard and Sharp (1996) suggest four alternative ways of structuring literature surveys and results: (1) chronological, (2) categorical, (3) sequential or (4) perceived importance. They demonstrate these options with the example of a study of how computer systems have affected marketing practice. These are the different options:

(a)   Chronological:

   1 Early history.
   2 The 1960s and 1970s.
   3 Recent developments.

(b)   Categorical:

   1 North America.
   2 Other developed.
   3 Developing world.

(c)   Sequential

   1 Market research.
   2 Market planning.
   3 Market decisions.

(d)   Perceived importance:

   1 Sales models.
   2 Advertising models.
   3 Planning models.

Your literature review may encompass more than one of these options, leading to a layered effect:

1   North America:

    1.1 Sales models.
    1.2 Advertising models.
    1.3 Planning models.

2   Other developed:

    2.1 Sales models.
    2.2 Advertising models.
    2.3 Planning models.

3   Developing world:

    3.1 Sales models.
    3.2 Advertising models.
    3.3 Planning models.

Howard and Sharp repeat the most important advice for students choosing a structure: find one that makes sense to you (the writer) and then get on with it.

Methods of generating a synopsis

Several different techniques are available to help you generate an outline for your first draft. Some are listed below, but Cryer (2000, pp. 225–33) also provides an extended discussion of this subject. Ideally, you will generate section headings for your own thesis and some idea of content, noting what each section will contain and how it will develop the overall 'storyline'.

Answering questions

One way to generate a contents list for your thesis is to list all the possible questions that your reader might ask and then arrange them into an order that the reader can follow logically. The example in Box 4.1 shows how it can be done for an introduction. Stay alert for other sources of questions:

1   What questions has your supervisor asked you?
2   What questions has your research raised so far?
3   What questions are you most interested in?
4   What do you get asked at social events?
5   What were you asked when you gave a seminar on the subject?

Free association

Rico (1983) outlines a free-association method that she calls 'clustering for structure'. You write the main topic in the middle of a piece of paper and then write words and topics around the central topic. Look at the words later and spot a paragraph that you can write from them.

BOX 4.1   Questions to be answered in an introductory chapter

Why have you chosen this particular subject?
How did you approach the study?
What actions did you take?
Who helped or advised you?
How have you organised the written and visual material in your dissertation?
In what way are the appendices relevant?
What kinds of bibliography are included and why?
Where are notes and references to be found?
Is there any background or scene-setting information that would help to put the subject into context?
What is the scope of your study?
Have you deliberately omitted some aspect?
What is your theme or argument within the subject area?
How are you going to progress it in the dissertation?
Which are your main avenues of enquiry?

(Source: Hamilton, 1990)

Cryer (2000, pp. 207–9) shows how key words and topics can be linked in a mind-map design. Mind maps can be used either as a note-taking technique or as a way of developing a synopsis. The main topics thus become chapters and the branches can become sections of each chapter.

Shuffling postcards

On separate pieces of postcard (or 'Post-its' or index cards) write either brief notes on separate topics that will be included in your thesis or details of questions to be addressed. Then find a large flat surface such as a carpet, a table or a desk. Lay out your pieces of card in a logical order and then move them around, experimenting with different orders until you see one that seems the best way to present all your material to your readers.

Software packages

Software packages can help you create outlines, and one even transforms a brainstormed diagram into a linear plan. These packages can be worthwhile, especially when used in conjunction with other methods, and they are developing rapidly. Ask around for what is currently available.

Write it without the data

I have known people prepare skeleton tables and specimen graphs before they set out collecting their data. 'I'll write it without the data,' they say. This can be a useful exercise for finding your structure and can provide a starting point. It can also help you think through aspects of statistical analysis. Following on from this, you can determine whether you are being too ambitious.

ACTIVITY 4.4

If you are stuck for ideas of how to proceed with brainstorming your thesis structure, you may simply need more practice at developing structures. Here is a simple exercise. Find four other PhD theses: two from your own department and two closely related to your subject from other institutions (through inter-library loan). Open each thesis and read the abstract *but nothing else*. Close the thesis. Then use one or more of the brainstorming methods above to draft a skeleton plan of how you think that thesis might look. Allocate an approximate number of words to the major elements of your plan. Then look at how the thesis writer did it. Say to yourself, 'My way is as good as theirs.' This 'contents game' can be played with any book, and can be made into a group game. One person brings a book, introduces it by reading the blurb and says how many chapters there are. The others try to emulate the structure. Points can be allocated for the closest, but the main aim is to raise awareness of different structures and outlines. When you are confident enough you can try to structure your own thesis.

Indexing and accessing material

Your draft structure will not be your final structure. One purpose of the draft structure is to allow your thesis to grow by osmosis but not grow out of control. It allows you to go about your daily business without having to take a holistic view every day. You can see the whole only at certain times, but if you know that you need 500 words on a specific topic then you can see it as a day's work.

The other purpose of your thesis structure is that it provides a guide for filing (rather than piling) your material *as you collect it.*

Woodford's reservoirs

Booth (1985, p. 1) reviews Woodford's method of using different coloured paper for each section of a traditionally structured scientific report. If you know what your sections are going to be – introduction, materials, methods, results, etc. – you can use, say, red paper for notes on results, white for the introduction, etc. Then, when you come to write the report, you can pull out all the white pages and work with them to write the introduction. I know of one student who used the coloured-paper method during her BA degree, allotting different-coloured paper for each module. Other people work through their notes with highlighter pens and have a similar code.

Using computer files

In the examples from Becker (1986) and Howard and Sharp (1996), on pp. 86–87, the numbering system used decimal places to indicate the level of the headings. Computer files can be created to match the sections. While researching this section I put data relevant to 'planning' into OU/4 and data relevant to 'organising material' into OU/5. When I created new files I amended my overall number plan (scribbled on an A4 piece of paper) accordingly. Later I switched material around, altered the structure and changed the part headings. I created new directories when I had completed each subsequent draft (OU1, OU2, OU3) and then edited the original OU directory files to create the next version.

I try to collect only material that I am fairly certain of using. I exploit it with the end product in mind. Reading and researching tend to be more effective if you have a sense of direction, if you know what you are looking for or have definite questions in mind. They are most effective when you know exactly where you are going to file that piece of data. There is only one key question: where will it fit into what I am writing?

Indexing

If your note taking is already under way when you decide on your structure, you will probably need to index your notes. Ideally, you will have kept your notes on one side of the paper (using the back for a later project) with wide margins, so that you can shuffle papers around without misplacing what is on the back. Keeping separate topics on separate sheets gives you a head start, but all is not lost if you have not done this. My method of indexing is to allocate numbers to all sections of my synopsis and then annotate my notes appropriately in the margins. I number each page of my notes and do an index by section number:

1   Introduction

    1.1 Choice of subject ... pages 4, 5, 6 (of notes).
    1.2 My previous work ... pages 13, 29, 35.
    1.3 Scope of this study ... pages 1, 7, 54.

Then I can pull out all the appropriate pages for writing the day's required number of words. Let us look at this process in more detail through the eyes of one accomplished writer:

> *I deal with huge amounts of material. Sometimes I despair at the amount of material. It means that I have got to get the structure right and then I can systematically work my way through the material. I read my material very carefully until I know roughly what it comprises, and at that point I work out a more detailed plan, by which I mean chapter by chapter, section by section and paragraph by paragraph. (By sections I mean a certain number of paragraphs before a gap, which is denoted by an asterisk; if it is a long chapter, each section is quite substantial, so I will do the writing section by section.) Then I go through my material very carefully and very slowly, assigning stuff to different paragraphs.*

To be really mundane, I sort out my notes into piles, section by section, then take the notes from the first section's pile and work out what my order of play for that section is going to be. I work out, say, the twelve paragraphs that are going to be in that section, and annotate my notes to show which bit of the notes is going into which paragraph for which section. I used to annotate with an array of differently coloured pens, but it was quite time-consuming putting pens down and picking them up. Now I use numbers for chapters and letters for paragraphs, so 3D written on my notes is the fourth paragraph in the third section. Then I create more piles, one per paragraph, or, if I'm running out of office space, a pile for two or three paragraphs.

Then I write the thing. I know what the overall point of each paragraph is going to be, but I don't know until I write it which piece will get more emphasis. I might throw out material that is not interesting enough or significant enough, so it's not absolutely programmed in that sense. It's sufficiently well planned so that I can make the best possible job of the writing, knowing that the questions of structure have been taken care of. To use a driving analogy, I don't want to be looking at the map when I'm actually driving.

The more unstructured the material, the trickier this stage can be. If you feel overawed by qualitative data, you could consult books that deal specifically with that subject (for example, Wolcott, 1990).

Appendices and footnotes

Students often ask what to put in appendices. The answer is: anything that halts the flow of your thesis. This might include:

1   Terms of reference (original instructions).
2   Material too detailed for speedy reading.
3   Specialist or technical data not suitable for all readers.
4   Letters that set up key parts of the project.
5   Source material referred to in the text.
6   Research tools (e.g. questionnaires).

Many of these decisions can be made after the first draft has been completed. Madsen (1983) advises keeping footnotes close to the main text in the first draft and then separating them in later drafts. Check your department's style guide on how footnotes should appear.

A referencing system

The text of your thesis will contain references to the work of other researchers, and your thesis will end with a bibliography of the works referred to. From the start you will need to set up a systematic and consistent referencing system, and your overall plan should include sufficient time at the end to ensure that *all* citations in the text have full and consistent bibliographical references (in whatever system is preferred by your department). This can be helped by carrying a reminder card:

1   Title of the book or journal.
2   Title of the chapter (if an edited collection).
3   Volume, number and date of the journal.
4   Exact spelling of the names of the author(s) and/or editor(s).
5   Place of publication.
6   Name of publisher.
7   Year of publication.
8   Library shelf number (for later checks).
9   Page number.

This important point is discussed in more detail in Chapter 5 ('Undertaking a topic review').

Conclusion

Try to develop an architect's vision of how your thesis will look. If you do not have this vision (or a big enough part of it) there is no driving force and there is nothing by which you can set targets.

Setting targets

> Begin with the date on which the paper is due and work backwards.
>
> (Hubbuch, 1989, p. 37)

Professional writers are devoted to completing projects on time. They produce the right number of words in the right place at the right time in the right form. They set themselves targets, estimate their daily word output and regularly assess cumulative word totals.

This book covers many aspects of planning elsewhere (see Chapter 3), but the target-setting aspect deserves further consideration from your perception of yourself as a *writer*. The purpose of a writer's plan is to construct manageable word targets for each day, each week, each month and each year. You also need to estimate the ratio of time you will spend on writing, rewriting, revision, corrections and extra drafts. One student emphasises this:

> *If I was doing my thesis now I would do it as a commercial undertaking. I would treat the university as a client and write a proposal of what I was going to do and how long each task was going to take. As a professional freelance writer, I have to cost jobs, and to do that I need a good idea of what is required. I don't want to end up working for six months on something that I'd thought was going to take two. I have to be in agreement with a client as to what is required, so I will invariably write them a detailed proposal with costs: specifying the number of words,*

the number and type of illustrations; allowing for liaison with production staff, designers and proof-readers; clarifying the target audience; and so on. Then we know what we are talking about.

As we have seen elsewhere in this book (for example, Howard and Sharp's table 2 in Chapter 3), there are many tasks that need to be allocated time. It is easy to underestimate the time that will be spent on certain tasks: getting feedback, making minor revisions, compiling a bibliography, checking references, checking figures, completing the preliminary pages (acknowledgements, contents page, abstract, etc.), and checking details of the bibliography. Many aspects of the writing process will take longer than you think. This is why it is important to follow your plan and construct an early first draft. Make notes of additional things you might do later if you gain extra time from somewhere else in your plan.

I think the problem with a large project is knowing where to stop. Writers should have a good idea of what they want to do. If you don't stick to your original plan and instead pull out another twenty or forty research papers, then you must recognise that it might take you a lot longer than you have prepared for. I think maybe many people are overambitious. They try to cram in all they know. The thesis isn't a work of art, it's merely a thesis. It doesn't have to be perfect. It just has to state a case.

This point was also made in Chapter 2, where the issue of what constitutes a research degree was discussed.

Inevitably, the issue of setting writing targets is inherently linked with issues of effective reading strategies. Effective reading is about (1) choosing something to read that you can write about, (2) asking the right questions about what you want from the reading, and (3) making your reading work for you in your writing. Reading and writing are not necessarily separate phases. They are interconnected parts of the writing process.

We cannot hold all that we read in our heads, so, at this level, we are activating the reading into writing rather than relying on memory. All reading should have the omnipresent question: 'Where will this reading fit into a written draft of my thesis?'

Rudd (1985) concluded that a major contributory cause of postgraduates' failure to write up in time was the lack of an overall plan. This meant that students spent far too long on each stage of the research, a problem compounded when supervisors were not sufficiently closely in touch with students to ensure that they were working steadily.

Buckley and Hooley (1988) studied management research students and reached the same conclusion: 'the early, clear definition of the topic and the development of realistic timetables and schedules were considered particularly important [... by respondents].'

The professional approach is to plan from the back. A writer's first questions are 'How many words?' and 'When do you want it by?' This leads to a production-oriented plan, which in turn convinces writers of the need for early first drafts which pare down the research to the essential. These early drafts will have gaps, of course, and plenty of questions to answer later *if there is time.*

The major activity in Chapter 3, pp. 62–65, was all about planning and scheduling your tasks. This is all part of the planning and scheduling work. Your institution or your supervisor may set targets for you: for example, a written report of 3,000 words every month, three pieces of assessed written work in the first year or a thesis proposal by a specific date. If not, sort out writing deadlines with your supervisor. Or, if necessary, set your own targets and monitor them yourself.

Rudd (1985) suggested that full-time PhD students should budget nine months for writing a science thesis and twelve months for an arts or social science thesis. In any sustained writing regime there is a limit to what you can do each day. Many professionals believe that five hours a day of creative writing is the limit and ten hours a day is counterproductive in the long term.

Dorothea Brande's classic book *Becoming a Writer*, originally written in the early 1930s, reminds us that most writers flourish on a simple, healthy routine with occasional time off for fun:

> Bursts of work are not what you are out to establish as your habit, but a good, steady, satisfying flow, rising occasionally to an extraordinary level of performance, but seldom falling below what you have discovered is your normal output. A completely honest inventory, taken every two or three months, or twice a year at the least, will keep you up to the best and most abundant writing of which you are capable.
>
> (Brande, 1996, p. 89)

Completing a writing project is immensely rewarding and powerful. Meeting realistic targets is an excellent source of fulfilment. But first you need your targets – the number of days for each task and then, when you are writing, an equation that relates the number of words to the number of days.

ACTIVITY 4.5

Return to the activity and planning work you did in Chapter 3. In the light of what you have considered here, review the amount of time you have allowed for writing.

Negotiating feedback

There's a limit to the number of times that a supervisor can come to a thesis with a fresh pair of eyes.

(PhD student)

With the spoken word the first version is often the last (except for television and radio, where editing takes place). In contrast, the written product can be improved, and feedback is your market research. Writing with feedback is the most powerful way to improve your writing – but only if your feedback process works. Sometimes it can go horribly wrong.

> *Even after getting feedback on academic writing for over ten years now, I can still feel defensive when I first read it. It is often tempting to say, 'Well, they didn't read this carefully enough,' or 'But they've missed the point completely.' Then I quickly realise that if I had made the point more clearly the feedback would probably not have been given. But it helps to have several commentators, so that you are not at the mercy of a potentially idiosyncratic reader. I ask only those people who appreciate the need for constructive feedback and will give it in the spirit in which it is invited. Some people will always try to score points when giving feedback and they are best avoided (even if they are your friends or family).*

ACTIVITY 4.6

Read Appendix 4.2, 'Revising with feedback', from *Writing with Power* by Peter Elbow (1981). Then answer the following questions.

1 Who do you know who is good at giving feedback on (a) structure, (b) content, (c) writing style, (d) proof-reading and (e) grammar?
2 What sort of feedback do you feel qualified to give?
3 How long will it take someone to read a draft of your thesis?
4 What sort of emotional involvement do writers have when a large piece of their work is being read and commented upon?
5 Would you like a reader's comments in writing, by telephone or face-to-face?
6 Should you act on feedback comments immediately or let them settle?
7 How many people should read it?
8 What happens if you get contradictory feedback?
9 Can you give feedback to yourself?
10 How will you fill in the time while your thesis is being read?
11 Is there any value in reading your writing aloud (on your own or with others present)?
12 Should you ask your partner or friends for feedback on your work?
13 Is it fair for a reader to read one chapter at a time?

If possible, discuss your answers with a colleague (or writing buddy) who has also tackled this exercise, and together try to answer the following key questions:

1 How will you organise the feedback on your thesis?
2 How much time and skill do you have to give feedback to others?

Feedback comments should probably come from people who are in the same readership group as those who will read the final product. It also makes sense that they should have your interests at heart. This rules out competitors and people you do not respect. It may also eliminate anybody who does not value your independence as a writer.

Understanding writer's block

> Get pen to paper, thought will follow.
>
> (Old newspaper saying, quoted in Fenby, 1970)

Writer's block, defined as 'the temporary or chronic inability to put words on paper' (Nelson, 1993, p. 1), has only recently become the subject of serious academic study. Here I shall bypass much of the theoretical background, best summarised by Leader (1991), and the dramatic and erotic dimensions of writer's block portrayed in films such as *Betty Blue* (1986), *Her Alibi* (1989) and *Barton Fink* (1991). Instead I shall try to be practical.

Major blocks can last for months or even years, but all writers are affected by minor blocks, if only for a day or two. Hall (1994) constructs an inventory of writing problems and offers some solutions in her excellent thirty-two page booklet for undergraduates. What follows is a summary of the literature, together with suggestions for overcoming any block.

Too complex

> We have a practical problem of putting complex thoughts down on paper. We know what we want to say but we have difficulty in deciding the exact direction in which we want the sentence or paragraph to go. There are too many choices. We may be trying to pack too much information into a sentence or paragraph, or we have too many digressional paths to pursue.
>
> (Smith, 1982, pp. 130–1)

Smith suggests writing down all you are thinking on paper and then trying to break it up into sentences or paragraphs – trial and error. The important thing is to get the ideas on paper and write down what the choices are.

Too many notes

'We have plenty of notes but don't know how to convert them into a thesis.' Some students find note taking so addictive that the more they do the harder it gets to go back to the scary task of writing. Taking notes is by no means a warm-up for the act of writing. It is a different skill. Nelson (1993, p. 87) says: 'The tortured graduate student might be better off warming up for her thesis by writing a short article on a related topic than by indulging in yet another Talmudic perusal of her notes.' Nelson advises postgraduates to spend the same amount of time on composition as on note taking, so that they become habitual writers as well as habitual note takers. Another solution is to bring your note taking and writing closer together, as one accomplished writer has done:

> I think note taking is as creative as writing because effectively you should be starting the creative process when you take notes. Say you're in a library with a book in front of you. It's not a random act that you've got that particular book out of 50,000 books – it's because of your work. When you're reading, your brain should be actively whirring away, assessing whether this book is relevant to the project you are working on. If it seems interesting and relevant, if there's some kind of spark, then go for it and take detailed notes. If there isn't a spark then don't. The process should be under way. That for me is always the huge argument in favour of taking notes rather than photocopying. I keep photocopying down to a minimum because it's a bit like tourists taking endless photographs but not really seeing the place.

It's all too much

> We are scared of the magnitude of the task. We realise the commitment involved and once we start with a few words we will commit ourselves along a path from which we cannot come back.
>
> (Smith, 1982, p. 132)

This problem is solved by breaking the task down into manageable sections through settling on a draft structure (see pp. 84–92) and setting sensible targets (see pp. 92–94). You then need to decide whether or not to go ahead. If you achieve your targets, you can reward yourself on a daily basis (for example, with chocolate, a drink in the pub, an episode of *Neighbours*) or on a monthly basis (a holiday, a special event, etc.). Or you can punish yourself for not attaining targets. Harris (1974) describes a case study of a student who aimed to write five pages of an undergraduate dissertation a week for ten weeks. The student placed $5 in each of ten envelopes and addressed them to an institution she particularly disliked. If she failed to reach her target in a given week, she had to mail an envelope to the dreaded institution.

Too exposed to criticism

> Sitting down to write is a risky business because writers open themselves to scrutiny. To overcome these fears, to take the risk of being thought below par, we have to trust our colleagues. But academic disciplines are organised in a way that undermines trust. Who can we trust with our working drafts?
>
> (Richards, 1986, pp. 108–20)

Possible solutions are to write for someone you know you can trust or to write as if it were a letter to a friend. Hubbuch (1989) is of the opinion that students should always write for fellow students. Other solutions are to assume a pseudonym that sounds as though it belongs to someone less perfectionist and more risk-taking than yourself. Or, better still, stress to yourself that you are writing an experimental draft. After all, even the finished article does not need to be a masterpiece.

Too good – no good

Lamott (1995, p. 116) has identified radio station KFKD (short for K-F*****) which is playing in stereo inside our heads when we sit down to write: 'Out of the right speaker in your inner ear will come the endless stream of self-aggrandisement, the recitation of one's specialness, of how much more open and gifted and brilliant and knowing and misunderstood and humble one is. Out of the left speaker will be the rap songs of self-loathing, the lists of all the things one doesn't do well, of all the mistakes one has made today and over an entire lifetime, the doubt, the assertion that everything that one touches turns to shit, that one doesn't do relationships well, that one is in every way a fraud, incapable of selfless love, that one has no talent or insight, and on and on and on.'

First of all you have to notice that the radio station is on. Then you have to find your own way of switching it off and engaging solely with your work. Lamott suggests all sorts of rituals – a small prayer, votive candles, breathing exercises – to find a way of hearing your story above the noise of radio station KFKD.

Not up to it

> We are worried that the product of our labours will not come up to some ill-defined standard. We have the ghost of a schoolteacher sitting on our shoulder, waiting to pounce on every error we make.
>
> (Smith, 1982, p. 132)

Academic writers often find it difficult to separate the creative stage of writing from the judgemental stage. The solution is to engage with early drafts as *creative* acts. Have more fun with what you write. Release your inner child. You can postpone the judgement and tidy up the writing later. For example, if we think through every sentence ... sorry ... if we try to write the perfect sentence before ... no, let me think again ... we would never complete a sentence if ... no, it's not right ... if we try to achieve perfection in our writing, we won't even complete a sentence. I got there in the end. It's not right but it'll do for now.

Can't hit the right tone

There may be confusion about the writer's role. We need to find a mask that fits us and allows us to write as well as we can' (Aitchison, 1994, pp. 250–1). The academic mask may not suit your mood. You are allowed to experiment with different styles in early drafts. You are permitted to amuse yourself. You can edit your draft later, making it more consistent and giving it a more mature academic style. The main aim is to find a tone that will get your first draft written.

Depression has set in

Depression is often anger turned inwards. Find a way of getting in touch with that anger through your writing. As Watson (1987, p. 43) points out, 'to be angry, for an author, is to be in luck'. Let the energy come out rather than be turned inwards. Write about what you are unhappy about. Write about how you feel about your thesis. Write your thesis.

Other things to worry about

While working on a thesis, it is possible that a major life event may occur – a death in the family, a relationship break-up, becoming a parent, etc. This may take precedence, occupy your thoughts and distract you from your thesis.

If events distract you from your thesis, you may still continue the writing habit by writing about things uppermost in your life – good things or bad things. Writing about problems or life events may help to clarify them for you and it could help remove them into the background for a while so you can work on your thesis again. L'Abate and Cox (1992) are pioneers of writing therapy rather than talk therapy. You do not need to meet a counsellor to write about what is happening in your life. (And you do not have to meet your supervisor to write a report.) Writing can take place at any time in any place (and there is no waiting list).

> *I was the most reluctant student. I spent my entire time wanting to give it up. But it got later and later and I still hadn't given it up. Even the best candidates seemed traumatised by the writing stage. I remember one thesis-writer making a joke about how overstretched and underpaid we were. He said that he had barely enough money to feed himself let alone pay for all the psychotherapy he needed along the way. Another friend of mine had a tee-shirt printed with the words 'Don't even ask about the thesis.'*

Gone stale

All enthusiasm for the thesis has disappeared and staleness has set in. Cryer (2000, pp. 212–24) outlines three techniques to cope with flagging motivation:

1   Talking things through with others.
2   Maintaining a healthy life style through diet and exercise.
3   Discovering the likely cause (for which she provides a useful diagnostic aid).

On the first point, talking it through with others, you may agree with a student in a study by Rudd (1985): 'Whenever I talk about it to anybody I get enthusiastic again.' I have often tape-recorded blocked writers, and have had some success, particularly for methodology chapters. 'Tell me what you did,' I start, and then I ask more specific questions until they are talking freely. The writer then transcribes the tape and has a starting point for a crude first draft. Alternatively, there are times when a writer needs to take a break or switch to another project.

Can't let go

Some people do not want to let go of the thesis because it will leave a huge gap in their lives when it is finally completed. They stall and drag it out.

If you are not certain about the next stage of your career, you may hold on to your thesis for longer than those who are sure of their next move. Develop a clear career plan which is dependent on change when your money or time runs out. Set a deadline. And recognise that letting go of a major piece of work does result in a bereavement-type effect. Musicians, sports stars and actors all experience a post-performance emptiness after the adrenalin has all been released. Work with it. Write about it. Create something to look forward to. Look forward to the day when you get your thesis out of the door. Write about how you visualise the next stage of your life.

Not in the habit

We are blocked simply because we are not in the habit of writing' (Smith, 1982, p. 132). Make writing a habit. Reread pp. 74–79. Make sure you write, even on the days when you do not want to write. If you need to kick-start the habit again after a break, find something relatively easy to write. Write about anything.

To summarise, many of these blocking problems have similar solutions: make writing a habit; stop when you have met your target and you know what is coming next; write for a supportive reader; create a peaceful setting; try something different; 'free-write' about anything; have fun and release your creative child; speak into a tape-recorder or write a letter to a friend. If you are still stuck, two books may be helpful. Victoria Nelson's *On Writer's Block* (1993) is an excellent source but it is not always available in the UK. A more accessible guide to discovering and recovering your creative self is *The Artist's Way* by Julia Cameron (1995).

Rewriting and editing

Rewriting is the essence of writing well – where the game is won or lost.
(Zinsser, 1994, p. 187)

The final draft of your dissertation will have to be written in good English with correct grammar and spelling. Any deficiencies in the detail may lead to the verdict of 'minor corrections', and poor presentation could prejudice examiners against you: 'I examined a thesis recently and the abstract had spelling and grammatical errors. Several pages, including those of the abstract, were so badly photocopied that some of the text was missing. I couldn't help but think that the student was not even trying to pass.' We have finally arrived at the detail of rewriting, editing and correcting. This can be seen as a separate stage: first you generate the text, then you tidy it up. The education system seems to teach us that rewriting is a punishment, but it can be the most enjoyable part of the process. The need to revise is not the sign of a bad writer. It is quite the reverse. In fact, you do not need to be a good writer; you need only be a good rewriter.

Traditionally, newspaper offices and publishing houses have divided the labour. A journalist writes an article and passes it to a sub-editor. An author writes a book and hands the manuscript to an editor, who in turn passes it on to a copy-editor. Copy-editors and sub-editors improve the text by spotting typographical errors, punctuation problems and grammatical weaknesses, by rewriting to improve the sense and by ensuring consistency. At a later stage a proof-reader checks for any remaining errors. An editor oversees the whole process. These are specialist jobs.

Some students pay a copy-editor to correct their thesis. Copy-editors usually work freelance and can be found through local publishers or local advertisements. However, this section assumes that you may want to become proficient yourself. Increasingly, with cost-cutting within the publishing business, there is pressure on authors to do their own copy-editing.

Reference books

I am always surprised by how few students are aware of the classic books of an editor's trade. The most comprehensive guides are *Copy-Editing* by Judith Butcher and *The Chicago Manual of Style*. These books will show you how to lay out quotations, when to indent paragraphs, the correct use of grammar, how to be consistent, common spelling mistakes, how to use ellipses, when to use italics and a thousand other things. Most working editors keep a selection of other specialist books. These include *Hart's Rules*, H. W. Fowler's *Modern English Usage* and *The Oxford Dictionary for Writers and Editors*.

Number of words

'Had I had more time I would have written less,' said Benjamin Franklin at the end of one of his letters. Most theses can be cut with very little loss.

Your department should set a word limit for your thesis (as was discussed in Chapter 2, pp. 20–21). Most word-processing packages will count words for you, but you need to develop a sixth sense for the number of words, so you can assess how your thesis is growing, and then, later, you can decide how much to edit. Look out for repetitious or irrelevant sections that can be cut entirely. Look out, too, for redundant words.

Barrass (1982, pp. 60–1 and pp. 72–3) lists more than 100 tortuous phrases that can be simplified: for example, 'postponed to a later date' (postponed), 'in actual fact' (in fact) and 'it would appear' (apparently). One of my common faults is overuse of the word 'the'. Consider this sentence: 'The farmer provides the fresh produce for the distributive trades and the raw materials for the processor.' It can be rewritten: 'Farmers provide fresh produce for distributors and raw materials for processors.'

Working on your manuscript

Black's *Writers' and Artists' Yearbook* has a key to the symbols used by proof-readers and copy-editors. It is worth learning these marks while working on your manuscript. (Classic annuals like the *Writers' and Artists' Yearbook* and Turner's *The Writer's Handbook* are also the best guides to the newspaper and magazine business.)

Goldberg (1991, p. 82) believes that reading aloud is an essential part of the writing process. It makes writers more aware of awkward structures, long sentences and parts where the writing does not flow. The Marx brothers provide a good case study for the importance of reading aloud to others. They toured the United States with comedy plays in the 1930s and changed their script daily in accordance with audience reaction. By the end of the tour their rewritten script could be converted into a classic film.

Consistency (house style)

Many universities' research degree regulations set down only minimal requirements for the style in which you write your thesis. You must check up on your own regulations before you start writing in earnest in order to ensure that you do not contravene any house style. Anything not specified in the house style leaves you to choose your own way of doing things, as long as they are consistent within the text. According to Butcher (1981, p. 33): 'Few readers notice whether dates are written "10th August, 1974" or "10 August 1974", but inconsistency in style will distract their attention from what the author is saying – even though they may not be conscious of what has distracted them.'

Lots of items benefit from consistent presentation. Your department may have a policy on layout and standardisation, known in the trade as a 'house style'. If not, see Allison (1997). What is it to be? Double quotation marks or single quotation marks? The 18th century or the eighteenth century? Nine or 9? Five kilometres per hour or 5 kph? The 1920s or the twenties? Per cent or %? Ten degrees centigrade or 10°C? Four yards or 4 yds? The technology department or the Technology Department? Mr. Brown or Mr Brown?

When reading your manuscript for detail you may wish to construct an A to Z grid, noting words where the spelling needs to be consistent: cliff top or cliff-top; coal mine or coal-mine; St Peter's Church or the Parish Church of St Peter; the river Thames or the River Thames; north Devon or North Devon; World War I or the first world war; Newcastle upon Tyne or Newcastle-upon-Tyne; and so on. Consistency can then be achieved by using the search command in your word-processing package.

Software packages

There are software packages which check grammar and spelling but they have their weaknesses. Reference books are more important, and they put you in a more powerful position. Most important, compile a list of things that you know you should look out for in your own writing (see 'Reading').

READING

On your next library visit try to read either Booth (1985, pp. 7–27) or Sternberg (1988, pp. 58–69). Both writers outline key rules for writing. Alternatively, you may prefer to look through one of the other key books on the detail of writing, for example Carey (1976), Strunk and White (1979), Kelsch (1981), Collinson *et al. (*1992), Aitchison (1994) or the latest edition of Judith Butcher's *Copy-editing*. Make a list of twelve key factors that do not come naturally in your writing – common faults that you will need to bear in mind when editing. Keep that list and refer to it when you correct your own work in future (but do not let it affect your production of early drafts). What matters is what you aspire to in your writing.

ACTIVITY 4.7

Try the activity suggested by Cryer (2000, p. 155), which is a useful workshop exercise to discuss the relative merits of the active and passive voices. Postgraduates are often in a quandary about whether to use the active voice ('I conducted an experiment …') or the passive voice ('An experiment was conducted'). Sternberg (1988, p. 65) votes in favour of the active voice: 'Expressions stated in the passive voice are harder to read and make for duller reading than expressions stated in the active voice. Whenever you use a passive construction, try to restate it as an active one.' However, some departments still treat use of the active voice as an act of insubordination.

Major criticisms of academic writing

To help me with this chapter I spoke with two specialists: an experienced newspaper sub-editor who works on articles written by academics; and an experienced publishing editor whose skills have been applied to academic books. Their views on academic writing were remarkably similar, and can be summarised under the following five headings.

Lack of coherence

> *Under the pressure of time, and a lack of strictness on the part of publishers, a good many academic texts I see are frankly at the first-draft stage. I think too many academics imagine they can turn out a book by writing at weekends, so they knock out a text and then hand it over. The second part of the process is ignored – refinement, signposting and clarification. Very often the material doesn't fit together well. It has got all the parts but the transition of ideas and the stages and sequences are not easy to follow. There are structural problems.*

> *Journalists work to a pyramid system. The nub of the article is contained within the introductory paragraph. The rest of the piece flows out from this introduction and should support the controversial point contained in the first paragraph. But for an academic an article is a voyage of discovery and you find the conclusion around the last paragraph. The best point is usually contained in this concluding paragraph. The result is a piece which seems to have a random construction and can often appear to be self-contradictory.*

Evolving from these points is a concern about the length and convolution of sentences. Cryer (2000, p. 156) summarises the Fog Index, a mathematical formula to help people think about this issue; if sentences are too long, with too many words of three or more syllables, the reader can lose sight of what the writer is trying to say.

Ambiguity

The classic work on ambiguity, William Empson's *Seven Types of Ambiguity*, is now in its third edition. It was originally written in 1929, shortly after Empson had been expelled from his Cambridge college for having contraceptives in his rooms. The seven types of ambiguity range from people reacting differently to the same piece of language (innuendo) to statements that are so obvious that the reader invents meaning (tautology). Reading Empson, you get a sense of how ambiguity can creep into almost everything unless you are careful.

> On a technical point, a great many writers would benefit from keeping an eye on their pronouns. Pronouns could often refer to three things, so they end up referring to none. It is good practice to go through the text and change every pronoun to what it [the pronoun] should refer to. Thomas Macaulay [the nineteenth-century British historian] did this. He nearly always gives a name. He was criticised for it, but he responded by saying that one of the bugbears of writing was 'the wandering pronoun'.
>
> (Empson, 1929)

Ambiguous words include 'his', 'her', 'it', 'they', 'he', 'she', 'this', 'that' and 'these'. If you do not believe me, try to fathom out this passage from the eighteenth-century classic *Tom Jones* by Henry Fielding:

Upon the whole, then, Mr Allworthy certainly saw some imperfections in the captain, but as this was a very artful man, and eternally upon his guard before him, these appeared to him no more than blemishes in a good character, which his goodness made him overlook and his wisdom prevented him from discovering to the captain himself.

(Fielding, 1963, p. 90)

Sexism

Casey Miller and Kate Swift's classic book *The Handbook of Non-sexist Writing for Writers* was first published in 1981, long enough ago for sexist writing to have become extinct. Except that it has not.

> *There is still a lot of use of the generic 'he'. Whenever I see 'he' I have a picture of a man in a grey suit. I take out 'he', unless it refers to a specific male person.*

There are two easy ways to avoid 'he': either pluralise the sentence or change the order of the clauses. For example:

1   *Original*. Old geography books depict the life and customs of the African in ways damaging to his dignity.
2   *Pluralising*. Old geography books depict the life and customs of African people in ways damaging to their dignity.
3   *Restructuring*. An African's dignity was impaired by the ways old geography books depicted life and customs.

Indirect writing

> *Academics are always full of 'ifs' and 'buts' and 'maybes' and 'might well bes' and 'furthermores' and 'we may see thats' and 'neverthelesses' and 'moreovers' and 'on-the-one-hands' and 'on the other hands'. They couch things in phrases that imply they are nervous of their position. Rather than stating things in a positive way they will use a double negative because they are so scared of saying things directly.*

Factual errors

> *I recently corrected the birth and death dates of Catherine the Great in one text. But most copy-editors now agree that it is the author's responsibility to get the facts right. Copy-editors can't afford to spend time on that.*

> *Regularly academics mention someone obscure and spell the name of the person incorrectly. To become a professional journalist you have to check facts.*

Other comments on academic writing

We all have our own pet concerns about the specifics of writing, and it is perhaps wise to learn your supervisor's personal hates at an early stage. It could be the poor use of apostrophes, split infinitives or ending a sentence with a preposition.

One gripe of mine is the neglect of hyphens in academic writing. Aitchison (1994, pp. 117–23) and Fowler's *Modern English Usage* have good sections on the importance of hyphens, particularly for linking compound adjectives. Hyphens change the meaning and remove ambiguity, especially when a compound adjective is split between two lines.

A little-discussed issue is *register*. Moving from compound abstractions into slang can jar upon the reader. Howard (1984) dedicates a chapter to these issues, explaining how written and spoken English are different kinds of register. His book is a good place to start if you have no awareness of this.

I have also heard many non-academics criticise the flippant use of exclamation marks in academic writing. Exclamation marks are too often used to seek attention or to say 'please laugh' or 'I'm not being serious' rather than for their true purpose. As Strunk put it, 'an exclamation-mark is to be reserved for use after true exclamations or commands' (Strunk and White, 1979, p. 34).

My namesake, Andrew Ward, explains this beautifully in his novel *The Blood Seed*. The book's hero recalls learning about punctuation from his teacher:

> I remember him explaining English punctuation as follows: a comma was a cloud of breath; a question-mark was a quizzical eyebrow; an exclamation-point was the spittle on a shouting man's chin; a period [full stop] was a nail upon which you hung a thought to dry.
>
> (Ward, 1985, p. 89)

Final checks

Barrass (1982, pp. 108–9) and Cryer (2000, pp. 237–8) provide lists for checking the final version of a thesis. Here are some of the last-minute ones:

1   Are the cover and title pages complete? Do they provide all the information required by external examiners?
2   Is the contents page included? Are the headings consistent with the headings and sub-headings in the thesis?
3   Is the abstract in the correct place?
4   Are there any spelling mistakes?
5   Are technical terms, symbols or abbreviations properly explained?
6   Are all the sources of information listed in the bibliography?
7   Are all figures, tables and pages numbered and in order?
8   Do you have the correct number of copies?

Conclusion

While a chapter like this can offer support and perhaps demystify some aspects of the writing process, ultimately the way to learn is by reading, writing and studying the end-product of writers you respect. Try to find role models from within your subject. Search for writers who inspire you. Read biographies and autobiographies of writers you admire. Go to places that confirm your life as a writer – workshops, readings, any place where writing is discussed. When you read a paper or book, take five minutes to assess the strengths and weaknesses of the writer's writing skills. Ask successful colleagues how they go about writing.

I have provided a few examples of quotations from interviews but obviously you are free to ask the same questions of writers you meet by chance (regardless of their discipline). 'How do you work?' 'Where do you work?' 'How do you organise material?' 'What do you see as the common errors in writing?' And so on.

I shall leave the last word to Goldberg (1991, p. 105):

Every morning as soon as you wake up, and each night before you go to sleep, say to yourself, simply and clearly, 'I am a writer' … Go ahead. Say it: 'I am a writer.' Practise saying it when people ask you what you do. You might feel like a complete fool. That is okay. Step forward and say it anyway.

References

Note that the Dewey classification number for writing skills is 808 in most libraries.

Aitchison, J. (1994) *Guide to Written English*, London, Cassell.

Allison, B. (1997) *Student Guide for Preparing Dissertations*, London, Kogan Page.

Applebee, A. (1984) 'Writing and reasoning', *Review of Educational Research*, 45 (4), pp. 577–96.

Barrass, R. (1982) *Students Must Write*, London, Methuen.

Becker, H. S. (1986) *Writing for Social Scientists*, Chicago, University of Chicago Press.

Black (annual) *Writers' and Artists' Yearbook*, London, A. & C. Black.

Boice, R. (1987) 'Is released time an effective component of faculty development programmes?', *Research in Higher Education*, 26, pp. 311–26.

Booth, V. (1985) *Communicating in Science: Writing and Speaking*, Cambridge, Cambridge University Press.

Brande, D. (1996) *Becoming a Writer*, London, Macmillan.

Buckley, P. J. and Hooley, G. J. (1988) 'The non-completion of doctoral research in management: symptoms, causes and cures', *Educational Research*, 30 (2), pp. 110–16.

Butcher, J. (1981) *Copy-editing*, second edition, Cambridge, Cambridge University Press.

Cameron, J. (1995) *The Artist's Way: A Course in Discovering and Recovering your Creative Self*, London, Pan Books.

Carey, G. V. (1976) *Mind the Stop*, London, Penguin.

Collinson, D., Kirkup, G., Kyd, R. and Slocombe, L. (1992) *Plain English*, Buckingham, Open University Press.

Cowley, M. (ed.) (1982) *The Paris Review Interviews: Writers at Work*, first series, London, Penguin.

Cryer, P. (2000) *The Research Student's Guide to Success*, second edition, Buckingham, Open University Press.

Dunn, R., Dunn, K. and Treffinger, D. (1992) *Bringing out the Giftedness in your Child*, New York, Wiley.

Elbow, P. (1981) *Writing with Power: Techniques for Mastering the Writing Process*, New York, Oxford University Press.

Empson, W. (1995) *Seven Types of Ambiguity*, third edition, London, Penguin.

Fenby, C. (1970) *The Other Oxford: The Life and Times of F. Gray and his Father*, London, Lund Humphries.

Fielding, H. (1963) *Tom Jones*, New York, Signet Classic.

Goldberg, N. (1991) *Wild Mind: Living the Writer's Life*, London, Rider Books.

Griffiths, M. (1994) 'Productive writing in the education system', *Psychologist*, October, pp. 460–62.

Hall, C. (1994) *Getting Down to Writing*, Dereham, Peter Francis.

Hamilton, A. (1990) *Writing Dissertations*, London, RIBA.

Hammond, R. (1984) *The Writer and the Word Processor*, London, Coronet.

Harris, M. B. (1974) 'Accelerating dissertation writing: case study', *Psychological Reports*, 32, pp. 984–6.

Hartley, J. and Branthwaite, A. (1989) 'The psychologist as wordsmith: a questionnaire study of the writing strategies of productive British psychologists', *Higher Education*, 18, pp. 423–52.

Hayes, J. P. (1984) *James A. Michener: A Biography*, London, W. H. Allen.

Howard, K. and Sharp, J. A. (1996) *The Management of a Student Research Project* second edition, Aldershot, Gower.

Howard, P. (1984) *The State of the Language*, London, Hamish Hamilton.

Hubbuch, S. (1989) *Writing Research Papers across the Curriculum*, second edition, New York, Holt Rinehart & Winston.

Kelsch, M. L. (1981) *Writing Effectively*, Englewood Cliffs NJ, Prentice-Hall.

Kingston, K. (1996) *Creating Sacred Space with Feng Shui*, London, Piatkus.

L'Abate, L. and Cox, J. (1992) *Programmed Writing: A Self-administered Approach for Intervention with Individuals, Couples and Families*, Pacific Grove CA, Brooks/Cole.

Lamott, A. (1995) *Bird by Bird: Some Instructions on Writing and Life*, New York, Anchor.

Leader, Z. (1991) *Writer's Block*, Baltimore MD, Johns Hopkins University Press.

Madsen, D. (1983) *Successful Dissertations and Theses*, San Francisco, Jossey-Bass.

Miller, C. and Swift, K. (1989) *The Handbook of Non-sexist Writing for Writers, Editors and Speakers,* second British edition, London, Women's Press.

Murray, D. (1984) *Write to Learn*, New York, Holt Rinehart & Winston.

Murray, R. (1997) '... "Lessons from the Teachers": Writing Workshops for Staff and Students', Writing Development in Higher Education Conference, Aberystwyth.

Nelson, V. (1993) *On Writer's Block: A New Approach to Creativity*, New York, Houghton Mifflin.

Plimpton, G. (ed.) (1982–8) *The Paris Review Interviews: Writers at Work*, series two to seven, London, Penguin.

Richards, P. (1986) 'Risk' in *Writing for Social Scientists*, ed. Howard Becker, pp. 108–20, Chicago, University of Chicago Press.

Rico, G. (1983) *Writing the Natural Way*, Los Angeles, Tarcher.

Rossbach, S. (1987) *Interior Design with Feng Shui*, New York, Dutton.

Rossbach, S. (1991) *Feng Shui*, London, Rider Books.

Rudd, E. (1985) *A New Look at Postgraduate Failure*, Windsor, SRHE/NFER-Nelson.

Rudestam, K. E. and Newton, R. R. (1992) *Surviving your Dissertation*, Newbury Park CA, Sage.

Seymour-Smith, M. (ed.) (1980) *Novels and Novelists*, London, Windward.

Smith, F. (1982) *Writing and the Writer*, London, Heinemann.

Spear, W. (1995) *Feng Shui Made Easy*, London, Thorsons.

Sternberg, R. J. (1988) *The Psychologists' Companion: A Guide to Scientific Writing for Students and Researchers*, Cambridge, Cambridge University Press.

Strunk, W. and White, E. B. (1979) *The Elements of Style*, New York, Macmillan.

Turner, B. (annual) *The Writer's Handbook*, London, Macmillan.

Ward, A. (1985) *The Blood Seed: A Novel of India*, London, Deutsch.

Watson, G. (1987) *Writing a Thesis*, Harlow, Longman.

Wolcott, H. (1990) *Writing up Qualitative Research*, London, Sage Publications.

Zinsser, W. (1994) *On Writing Well*, fifth edition, New York, HarperCollins.

Appendix 4.1   Twenty-six ways to start writing

A promise: If you write until your hair's white, your eyes make the print blur, and your hands tremble on the typewriter keys, it will still be hard to start writing.

Writing reveals us to ourselves and eventually to others, and we do not want to be exposed on the page. The writing is never as good as we hoped, so it is natural that we resist this exposure. We have to find ways to get over this understandable psychological hurdle, this normal stage fright before the blank page.

Writing is also a commitment. Once we have put down one line, sometimes just one word, we have made a choice, and the direction of our writing, its limits, its pace, its dimensions, its voice, its meaning are all constrained. Everything is not possible.

The process approach described in this book is itself an attempt to get us writing in a normal way. We collect material, focus it, and order it. At least 60 percent of our time and effort is spent in planning and preparation for writing so that we will be ready, often eager, to make a run at the blank page. If we aren't ready to write it may mean that we need to go back to collect, focus, or order.

Experienced writers, however, still find it hard to get started writing. Here are some of the tricks they use:

1. Make believe you are writing a letter to a friend. Put 'Dear ———' at the top of the page and start writing. Tom Wolfe did this on one of his first New Journalism pieces. He wrote the editor a letter saying why he couldn't write the piece he'd been assigned. The letter flowed along in such a wonderful, easy fashion that the editor took the salutation off and ran it. It established a new style for contemporary journalism.

2. Switch your writing tools. If you normally type, write by hand. If you write by hand, type. Switch from pen to pencil or pencil to pen. Switch from unlined paper to lined paper, or vice versa. Try larger paper or smaller, coloured paper or white paper. Use a bound notebook or spiral notebook, a legal pad or a clipboard. Tools are a writer's toys, and effective, easy writing is the product of play.

3. Talk about the piece of writing with another writer, and pay close attention to what you say. You may be telling yourself how to write the piece. You may even want to make notes as you talk on the telephone or in person. Pay attention to words or combinations of words that may become a voice and spark a piece of writing.

4. Write down the reasons you are not writing. Often when you see the problem you will be able to avoid it. You may realize that your standards are too high, or that you're thinking excessively of how one person will respond to your piece, or that you're trying to include too much. Once you have defined the problem you may be able to dispose of it.

5. Describe the process you went through when a piece of writing went well. You may be able to read such an account in your journal. We need to reinforce the writing procedures that produce good writing. A description of what worked before may tell us that we need to delay at this moment, or it may reveal a trick that got us going another time. We should keep a careful record of our work habits and the tricks of our trade, so that we have a positive resource to fall back on.

6. Interview other writers to find out how they get started. Try your classmates' tricks and see if they work for you.

1

7. Make writing a habit. For years I started every day by putting a pocket timer on for fifteen minutes and writing before I had a cup of coffee. Now the timer's not necessary. When writing, any kind of writing, is a normal activity, it's much easier to start on a particular writing project. You are used to spoiling clean paper the same way joggers are used to wearing out running shoes.

Appendix 4.2 Revising with feedback

Revising with feedback is the most powerful way to revise, and happily enough it is also the most interesting and enjoyable technique. No-revising relies on a magical polishing process inside you – using luck and your unconscious. Quick revising relies on a detached critical consciousness: you step out of your involvement with your writing and clean it up with dispassionate pragmatic eyes; you can make quick harsh decisions because you haven't got time to vacillate, you must cut your losses. Thorough revising relies most of all upon time – more time for careful wrestling and more time in addition for setting your writing aside, which gives you newer, fresher eyes than you could get by mere will power or any vow to be dispassionate. Cut-and-paste revising … relies on aesthetic intuition. When you revise with feedback you are of course trying to use all these faculties, but in addition you are using the most powerful tool of all: the eyes of others.

How much feedback and when

You can bring feedback into the revising process either early or late. If you bring it in early you are in effect using the reactions of others as part of the very process of making up your own mind. If you bring it in late, you are reaching all your conclusions alone but using the reactions of others to help you make those conclusions *work* better on readers.

You will want to hold off on feedback till the end if you are in a hurry or if you know you don't want to make any changes in your thinking or if you are nervous about using feedback. In these situations you get feedback only once and you use it only for making minor or cosmetic changes. But bring feedback in early if you want the most powerful and interesting process and have time. It means getting feedback on two or more drafts and inviting others to be part of a slower and more organic process as you work out your thinking.

Here's how this longer process might look. You start by producing a draft. It's probably something you've long wanted to work on, something important to you, not something you have to force yourself to write for a deadline. You revise it enough to make it interesting and readable, but you aren't trying to make it your best work. You don't spend much time revising it and it probably doesn't represent your final thinking. (Cut-and-paste revising is especially useful here.) It probably has serious problems of structure and consistency. But it must be readable.

You get two friends to read it and then you sit down with them. You are more interested in their thoughts on the whole matter than their criticisms of your writing. Why try to fix weaknesses when you will probably take a whole new approach on your next draft? The conversation with them helps you see the whole thing in better perspective, gives you new ideas, and helps you make up

2

your own mind what you think. Your draft was really just a letter to friends exploring your thinking.

On the basis of this first step of informal feedback you can 're-see' the whole thing and write a brand new draft—not just strengthen that first draft.[1] On this draft, too, your main priority is not to try to get it right, perfect, make up your mind once and for all (unless you are in a hurry and know you have to stop with this draft). You are trying to let the whole thing develop slowly through your interaction with others. Wait patiently for things to jell. Again, you get readers to give you feedback on this draft: perhaps the same readers, perhaps new ones. And here, too, you are interested in all their thinking on the topic, not just their reactions to your writing. At this point things may click and it may be very clear to you how you want your final draft to go; but perhaps not. You may take it through this process once or even twice again depending on your time and on how much you care.

Indeed, other people's feedback can lead you to a whole new understanding of the writing process so you develop a much longer time frame. That is, perhaps the feedback you get on this second round is very confusing: each reader has entirely different reactions, feelings, suggestions. You know your piece of writing isn't right yet, isn't done, but you are unclear about what changes to make. Perhaps you realize it could evolve in two very different directions but you don't know which you prefer. But you also know it's already good. Good enough, if you just polish it slightly, that others will want to read it; good enough perhaps even to publish. You are not done in the long run, but you know you have carried it as far as you want for now. You need to give it time to settle, give yourself time to have new thoughts and experiences and grow into a slightly different person. Then months or even years later you come back to it. You revise it and finally get it right.

I have let my story of a typical case of revising with feedback stretch into an extreme case. But the point I want to make is that when you revise with feedback, you develop a looser and more conditional sense of what it means to be 'done'. Instead of a clear one-step change from *rough draft* to *final draft* – from raw to cooked in one transaction – you are allowing a gradual evolution through time and through successive audiences. At each stage you can call your draft 'done' or 'not done' depending on how you want to use it. On the one hand you start using the word 'done' early: you learn to polish slightly and re-type even your earliest drafts so that they are useful for others to read. But on the other hand, you learn to think of things as 'undone' on into late drafts since you know that hearing the reactions of others can trigger continued growth even when you thought your mind was made up.

Enormous benefits flow from this odd flexibility about when to call something done. You aren't always struggling for perfection, worrying 'Do I really know enough yet?' Instead of wrestling to get it right on the first try, you experiment without anxiety on different approaches and *wait* for the right way to pop into your mind. It will. There's a wonderful deep thud you feel when your meaning finally drops into place – just what you wanted to say – which is hard to achieve without trying out a draft or two on real readers and feeling how they understand your words.

Perhaps it seems as though this approach allows for too much indecision. I hear a tough person saying, 'There's something wrong with all this tentativeness.

3

Damn it, you can't write unless you learn to make up your mind.' Which is true. Writing *is* a process of making up your mind, and much bad writing is bad because the writer didn't have the guts to do so – or because he made up his mind but still had inner doubts which fog up his writing and prevent him from asserting his conclusion crisply. The point is, though, that most people make up their minds better if they do so gradually without being under too much pressure.

This method of successive drafts not only helps you be more decisive in your final draft, it also helps you write more decisively on early drafts. You aren't committed to what you write on early drafts, so you don't have to hedge and be cautious. You find it easier to use bold strokes and definite language – to avoid the mumbling qualifications and maybe's that destroy strong writing. And sometimes you discover that an interesting hunch is true only because you permitted yourself to overstate it, go with it, and thereby discover arguments and evidence you never would have thought of if you had remained judicious.

Once you start enjoying the power of this slower interactive way of revising, you will learn to use it for other writing, not just pieces you want to write for yourself at a relaxed pace. You will learn to handle deadlines differently. If you have a month, you will be eager to use this new leverage of feedback and get yourself to produce an exploratory draft in a week so there are three more weeks for feedback and more drafts. Even if you only have a week, you will discover that you can dash off a draft tonight – since the pressure is off – and get at least one round of feedback and discussion before you have to figure out what you really think.

Your decision about when to bring in feedback, then, turns out in the end not to depend so much on *time* as on how much you want of that creative mess in which you let the thinking of others get all mixed up with your own. Here is a schematic summary of your options:

1. *Minimal feedback.* You should *always* use feedback to help you eliminate errors in grammar and usage from any final draft that needs to be polished – no matter what kind of revising you engage in. But don't let them talk about what you are saying or how you say it – just spelling, grammar, and usage.

2. *Little feedback.* You don't have much time or you don't like feedback or for some reason you want to keep others largely out of your writing process. You get one round of feedback only at the end, and you know you will stick with your conclusions no matter what they say. But you can still get enormous benefits from their reactions. Even if they happen to think you are dead wrong in one of your major ideas, their objection will help you make improvements in how you present that idea. For example:

- explain the idea entirely differently,
- insert a needed clarification or defense,
- remove a troublesome example or detail,
- put the idea in a different place in your whole structure.

And their reactions will help you make other small but important changes:

- remove bits that don't work,
- untangle some snarls in language or logic,
- change an annoying tone of voice here and there,
- insert some little introductions or transitions or clarifications that may make all the difference in the world to a reader's staying with you or not.

4

'Please find mistakes in spelling, grammar, and usage; and any awkward or unclear sentences. Don't tell me if you dislike or disagree with my thinking. I haven't got the time or strength for any major rewriting. But please point out places where you think I make an absolute fool of myself.' This is a feedback request I sometimes make of my wife – usually at the last minute.

3. *Medium feedback*. Your mind is made up about your main message. You aren't willing to give yourself the grief of rethinking your position entirely, but you are willing to engage in *major* revisions of structure and strategy. Perhaps you argued your case through abstract reasoning, but feedback convinces you it's worth trying to do it almost entirely through example or anecdote. Perhaps feedback convinces you that you have to turn your whole structure upside down. Usually your revisions are less drastic. Once you understand what is confusing or bothering a reader, it is usually not too difficult to find a way to deal with the problem.

4. *Lots of feedback*. Everything is up for grabs from the beginning. You share drafts from the start – before you know your thinking. You let the interaction carry you on a voyage of discovery.

The crucial thing is to decide how much of the feedback process you want. As I finish typing on this sheet of paper and take it out of the typewriter and put it face down on the pile to my right, I am reminded of how sometimes I don't want much. For I notice on the back (I usually write on the back of already used paper); it says 'Draft III, FSU, DR, p. 17.' This is the third draft of a chapter David Riesman wrote about a competence-based program at Florida State University and circulated to readers for feedback. And yet I am on at least the third draft of this chapter now and haven't let anyone see what I've written. (I will get some feedback before I finish with it.) Sometimes, in short, I just want to work out my ideas myself. 'I can do it my *own self*,' says Abby, age three, as I start to help her with something difficult and she pushes my hands roughly away.

But Abby's phrase is ominous too. For sometimes after she has pushed me away, she must come back sheepishly and ask for help. And so have I numerous times had to put a draft through a major change later on after I thought it was settled but late feedback shows me I'm wrong. I fight the change harder when I've already invested so much work and made up my mind. It would have been easier if I had been willing to bring in feedback earlier. On other pieces of writing – where I feel more secure or unpossessive – I'm comfortable with bringing in feedback from the start.

You may be surprised by a powerful side effect of using feedback for revising – especially if you bring in feedback early. You may find that after years and years of strenuous but unsuccessful efforts to make your writing clear for *real* readers – teachers, employers, editors, strangers – all of a sudden you can write much more clearly now that you are just cleaning up a rough draft for a friend to read and respond to. You aren't even trying to make it your best writing yet your language turns out clearer, simpler, more direct. Once you realize that your reader is a friend and helper, sometimes you cut right through that abstractness or complicatedness or fog that has plagued you for so long. The important point psychologically is that when we write for 'real audiences' like teachers and employers, the stakes are very high and we get too clenched. What's more we are liable, without realizing it, to feel the reader as *enemy*. After all, they *are* the enemy: they've hurt us deeply time and again in the past, the dirty bastards.

5

When, on the other hand, we feel the reader as genuine friend and ally, suddenly words flow more easily and humanly. This effortless change of audience can do more than all your strenuous wrestling in the past.

Your main task in getting feedback is to listen and see if you can experience what your reader is experiencing. If you succeed in doing so you will be able to see whether there's really something there to fix and if so how to fix it. Try being totally silent after you ask a few questions. Avoid the temptation to keep talking about what *you* had in mind; try discovering what you got into *their* minds. Try *believing* your readers: not so you are stuck with their view forever, but so you can see your writing through their eyes. You are not yet trying to make up your mind about anything, you are trying to enlarge your mind. You probably made up your mind as you wrote your draft so in a sense you are trying to unmake your mind. ...

The essential skill in all revising is the ability to look at your own writing and see potentialities: see what is almost there or sort of there or even to see what is not there at all but ought to be. It is like the ability to look at a room and see how it *could* look with different furniture differently arranged. More specifically you need:

- to see what the words don't yet say but want to say,
- to see a potential shape that's not yet there but which would make everything click,
- to see a simple way to say something that's now roundabout,
- to see bits you can leave out, even though you love them.

Time, intuition, and a detached critical consciousness are obviously helpful tools if you want to look at your writing and see what could be there. But nothing is so powerful as a chance to see your words through the eyes of others.

Note

1   Occasionally, of course, you find that you stumbled on to the right idea and the right structure the first time and so now you are just improving that first draft rather than writing a completely new one.

Acknowledgements

I would like to thank all those who either commented on the manuscript or agreed to be interviewed: Barbara English, Jacqueline Eustace, Ruth Finnegan, Penny Gray, Jacky Holloway, Anne Horner, Lynn Jones, Helen Kemp, David Kynaston, Martin Le Voi, Rose Lonsdale, Chris Murray, Stephen Potter and Piers Worth. Grateful acknowledgement is made to the following for permission to reproduce material in the appendices: Holt Rinehart & Winston for Appendix 4.1, from D. Murray, *Write to Learn* (1984); Oxford University Press for Appendix 4.2, from Peter Elbow, *Writing with Power: Techniques for Mastering the Writing Process*, copyright © 1981 by Oxford University Press: used by permission of Oxford University Press Inc, New York.

Chapter 5

Undertaking a Topic Review

Stephen Potter

After reading this chapter you will be able to:

- **Establish the purposes for which you are undertaking a topic review**

- **Plan and organise your topic review**

- **Identify sources of information**

- **Document your topic review**

- **Arrange information-search training**

- **Write up your topic review**

Although this chapter does contain some general advice on the practicalities of finding literature and other sources, the main focus is on planning a search and the research purposes of undertaking a topic review in your subject area. If you are not familiar with the practicalities of information searching (and the technology is moving fast), you must sort them out in conjunction with using this chapter. Your supervisors should be able to book you on a training course; if not, it is worthwhile contacting the person responsible for knowledge retrieval/information searching at your library, who will be able to help you with training. Part-time students should also have access to their university's training facilities. In addition, most public libraries today have staff specialising in IT who can provide information searching advice.

If you are otherwise unable to obtain training in the practicalities of information searching, The Open University Library website has public access to online training. You can access this via the OU Library's home page (http://oulib1.open.ac.uk/) or via the 'ROUTES' page that supports the OU version of this training material (http://oulib1/open.ac.uk/ROADS), press 'Browse' and scroll down the OU courses to U500 and look at the 'Section 10' entry. The latter also provides links to some key databases.

Your supervisors may also suggest other information guides appropriate to your subject area. One guide, in the Sage *Study Skills* series, that covers the social sciences is: C. Hart *Doing a Literature Search* (2001) Sage Publications, London. In this section, any reference to an *Information Search Guide* will mean whatever guide you are using. You are expected to use your Information Search Guide to learn the practicalities of finding information in your subject area.

Reviewing your topic area is a major activity for any research degree. Depending on your previous experience in information searching, this section will take at least 10 hours to complete, including undertaking some basic literature-searching activities. In addition to this, you will certainly need to refer to this section again at several points in undertaking your research project.

The purposes of a topic review

A 'literature review' forms a crucial part of any research degree or dissertation. Increasingly, not only literature is involved but also other forms of information (particularly electronic). Basically, for several reasons, what you need to find out is 'where things are at' – however the 'things' are documented. The terms 'topic' or 'state of the art' are used when reviewing 'where things are at', so the term 'topic review' is used here. However, please note that when reference is made to other people's work the term 'literature review' will also be used. In most cases it will have the wider meaning embodied in the phrase 'topic review'. When *only* literature is concerned, it will be made clear. Sorry about this, but the terminology is changing!

It is essential to think through carefully the purposes of a topic review.

There is no point in simply wading into the literature and other contacts thinking you can 'immerse' yourself in your subject. Particularly today, when information systems are so powerful, there is an immense danger of simply being overwhelmed by the vast volume of information that is out there.

In your research you will need to draw upon what other people have done at several points, at differing depths and for different purposes. Although your thesis or dissertation is likely to have a chapter headed 'Literature review' (or 'Topic review', 'Subject review' or 'State-of-the-art review'– whatever you call it), this is not the only place where you will need to show an understanding of what others have done on your chosen topic area.

ACTIVITY 5.1

Note down what purposes will be fulfilled for your research project by reviewing the topic. How will you use the literature and other information? How will you document it? Make a list, plus any brief notes you think are necessary. The list will be used later in this chapter.

Conceptions of a topic review

To follow on from this activity I shall use the work of an Australian education researcher, Christine Bruce (1994). She surveyed Master's and doctoral students in the early stages of their research projects and asked them to reflect on what they understood a 'literature review' to be. The students came from a wide variety of academic disciplines. From their responses she developed a typology of six conceptions of a literature review (a term that covers the broader definition we have called a 'topic review'). These conceptions were:

1   *The literature review as a list*: a collection of discrete items on a particular subject, possibly with keywords or a short description.
2   *The literature review as a search*: identifying information that is useful for a research project.
3   *The literature review as a survey*: investigating writings and research to discover the knowledge base and the methods of investigation used.
4   *The literature review as a vehicle for learning*: using the literature as a sounding board to check out the researcher's ideas and perceptions of a subject; seeking to gain understanding derived from reading the literature.
5   *The literature review as a research facilitator*: helping develop a particular stage of the research process; for example, on a particular methodology, on refining the research question, when something unexpected has happened and the research needs to take a new direction.
6   *The literature review as a report*: a written discussion of previous investigations.

Your list of purposes in Activity 5.1 may or may not map on to this typology (you may have responded to the question in a different way), but see whether you can slot your list of the 'purposes' of a topic review into Bruce's categories. Write the above list numbers next to the items on your list. (You may end up with something in more than one category, and if there is a 'main' one, underline it.)

The purposes of a topic review

A major conclusion of Bruce (1994) was that, in the early stages of research, postgraduate students tend to have a 'list', 'search' and 'survey' concept of the literature/topic review, but that:

> students' thinking needs to be challenged as early as possible in their research programme so that it is clear that the final product of the literature review is a coherent synthesis of past and present research. It is not a list or annotated bibliography on the area of interest, although these may represent early stages in progress towards the end product.
>
> (Bruce, 1994)

Your understanding of what others have done must inform your own research; eventually you will show where your research fits into the body of knowledge of which it is a part.

There is one point that Bruce does not emphasise. It is the simple practicality that your purposes of reviewing literature will change as you progress through your research. It will help you if you are alert to all you may need from the literature and other sources of information. For example, you may be more interested in understanding the results of a piece of work in the early stages of your research, of the research method used once you start thinking about your own data gathering, and perhaps why there are differences between your results and those in the literature when your data are gathered in. Look back at Chapter 1, where Figure 1.1 shows the links between the 'state of the art' topic review and other tasks in a research project.

One postgraduate commented:

> *I have learned how one's review of the topic changes and grows. I have probably tried three-plus versions of it by now, and it is still changing. It will change, grow, expand and deepen over time. This movement is a good sign. Several writings may actually be part of the process of achieving the understandings wanted from the review.*

The following list of purposes is based on a variety of sources, including Bruce's 'conceptions' and research training experience at a number of universities in Britain by the team that have put this book together. Nevertheless, you may have additions of your own.

1   To gain knowledge on the subject area. This is a matter not only of finding out what are the major research issues and debates, but also of developing your ability to appraise critically what others have done. Who has done interesting work? Why do you think their work is good?

2   To find out where the literature is thin, or where there are gaps in the knowledge. It is important to note not only what research has been done, but also what has not been adequately researched.

3   To gain feedback information in order to rethink and focus a research topic. This concerns sorting out key issues and 'hot' research topics and assists you in formulating or refining your core research question.

4   To find out whether there are related or parallel literatures that have developed in isolation. Information or method from one area could help another. For example, a research student looking at the work of private consultancies commissioned to help develop the EU Ecolabel noticed that they had failed to take account of closely related energy studies and methodologies developed in government research labs in the United States. Two related literatures had developed in isolation from each other.

5   To discover *how* others have researched the chosen topic area. Look at literature and other sources to explore methods, research questions, data availability and analysis as well as results.

6   To justify how and why you have done the research in the way you have. For example, one OU student used a hybrid case study/modelling method in his transport research because he felt that models on their own were inadequate. Other researchers had reached a similar conclusion which supported this important decision.

7   To have a body of information to compare with your research findings. When reporting and discussing your results you need to compare them with what other researchers have found out.

These purposes are relevant to all postgraduate degrees (although a taught Master's dissertation or BPhil may not have original research findings). However, the depth to which they are pursued will vary according to the criteria for a Master's dissertation and for each research degree (which were discussed in Chapter 2).

Broadly, at an appropriate level for each degree, examiners will expect students to have used their knowledge of the topic to show that:

1   The researcher knows his or her subject.

2   The researcher has undertaken a critical review of other work in the field – not just a list, but a demonstration of understanding. Think of it as providing a guided tour of a topic, pointing out important features (not every insignificant molehill).

3   The researcher knows the relationship of his or her work to the rest of the field; for example, is it supported by and/or does it extend what other researchers have done? Does it add new meaning to what others have done? Does it break new ground?

Discussion

Alan Woodley's review in Appendix 5.1 is certainly a critical appraisal – he notes what other researchers have done and says that one line of investigation appears to be more

ACTIVITY 5.2

Read Appendix 5.1, 'Reviewing the literature', by Judith Bell, at the end of this chapter. It focuses in particular on the production of a critical review of existing work in your topic area. Read as far as the end of the excerpt from Alan Woodley. This is about educational research, but it is written so that anyone should be able to comment on how good it is as a critical literature review. Having considered the purposes of a topic review, list which of them Woodley's review fulfils. When you have done this, read Bell's last paragraph.

satisfactory. The review also shows that he was using information to rethink and focus on a core research question and to explore how others have researched in this area. Method is a key component of this review, and the work Woodley has done specifically emerges from an approach in the literature that he considers to be most valid. In this introduction he does not report his findings, but clearly he has a body of information to compare with his own results.

Method, focus and comparison

A critical assessment of the work of others should become the springboard for your own work. Your own programme of research should emerge (as it did in Alan Woodley's case) from showing that a particular aspect requires attention and that you are the person who is going to do it.

However, you will need to draw upon your knowledge of the subject area throughout your research work, not just in order to set it up. This links with Bruce's 'higher' purposes of a review: as a 'vehicle for learning' and 'research facilitator'. Put simply, as you progress in your research project you will need to draw upon the work of other people to help you:

1   Identify the methods of investigation used.
2   Focus on the exact research problem or question you will address.
3   Sort out problems that emerge.
4   At the end of your thesis, to compare your results with those of others to show how and where your contribution has taken place.

In particular, relating your own work to what others have done is an important hallmark of a good research degree, yet often a topic review is seen only as a 'scene setter'.

Writing a review

Students often have difficulty in starting to write their topic reviews. There is a feeling that you have to collect everything first before you can do it. Especially when using on-line, internet or CD-ROM searches, the searching process itself can become almost obsessive. It is actually much better to start writing immediately. This point is emphasised in Chapter 4, 'The writing process', which is a very important part of this book. You should study it early on in your research work. Writing is a continuous process throughout your research degree, not a separate stage at the end.

There are specific sections of Chapter 4 on getting started and getting into the habit of writing. The following ideas are in addition to the general guidance found in Chapter 4.

I got one of my full-time PhD students to write a review of just ten pieces of literature when he was two months into his PhD. The ten pieces were reasonably central to his subject area, but he did not spend ages narrowing down a vast list to 'the ten crucial works'. They were simply ten that looked promising at the time. It was surprising how reviewing these ten pieces developed his sense of discernment in looking at other literature. Having completed a 'mini-review', he could judge rapidly the value to his project of subsequent articles. In consequence, doing this quick and incomplete review speeded up his whole topic review. The initial review was quickly superseded, but evolved into a series of reviews covering the purposes discussed above. This student later became a professional journalist.

Another way of getting going on your review is linked to the level and depth of knowledge needed as you focus on your core research question. Writing up the general subject area and the main issues of debate should be a relatively straightforward task. It does not require too much depth and is also something that many other researchers will have done. Try finding somebody else's general review in your subject area and examine it critically. For example, research into a detailed aspect of renewable energy sources (say, small-scale wind generators) will need to start off by discussing why renewable energy is an important issue and the environmental concerns behind its development. This general subject is covered by many articles and books.

Although you obviously must not simply appropriate another person's review for yourself (that is not ethical – see Chapter 7), a useful exercise is to work out how you might adapt the review to make it better suited to your own purposes. It can then form the basis of structuring your own general review.

Locating sources

Any information search guide will provide an overview of the major sources of information in a particular subject area. Surveys also appear from time to time in journals and professional bodies (for example, the Institution of Mechanical Engineers produces Sourcebooks and Information Packs. Some of these sources are contained in Routes) (see p. 12). Do ask your supervisors about key sources.

Make a note of the main sources of information so far in your studies and compare them with the sources in the information search guide you are using. For example, one student noted:

Before I applied to do my PhD I had read a couple of articles in relatively serious practitioner journals which really inspired me to think about the area I was interested in and to want to investigate it further. A lot of the references in them seemed relevant too and as soon as I started the PhD I got hold of the further articles concerned. This combined set of 'key articles' stood me in good stead throughout the research, leading me to more detailed literatures and identifying important names in the field (many of whom I later met at conferences, etc.).

This was certainly a good way to get going on sources, but equally there is a danger of using only a certain set of sources with which the student may be familiar (for example, a particular group of journals, a reading list supplied for a course, the reference list of a good article or a particular on-line database).

Conversely, information searching is not just a matter of mechanically working through all possible sources to obtain everything ever written containing certain key words. You must be selective and realistic about your search, hence the points made above about writing up as you go, and also discussing your searching strategy with your supervisor. Starting off like the student in the example above is fine, but at some point you must do a more systematic search.

ACTIVITY 5.3

1   If you are unfamiliar with information searching using an information search guide, find an example of a search and simply repeat it, using an on-line or CD-ROM database.
2   Using an information search guide appropriate to your research subject, do a search to identify just two articles and two books on a specific topic associated with your research.
3   Repeat the search to see whether you can identify any sources that provide an overview of your topic area.

People and networks

People as informants

Literature (in either its paper or its electronic form) is not the only way to find out about the topic area in a particular subject. Indeed, probably the quickest way to find 'where things are at' is to ask someone 'in the know'. Talking to people who are very familiar with the topic area is an excellent way to speed up finding out who has done what. This does not replace searching and analysing written sources, but it can very much help you to identify what is viewed as important work and help you to select key work and key researchers.

An example was an OU postgraduate student who, in the first few months of his PhD, sought to interview several key people in his field of study. He purposely chose a mix of researchers, practitioners and journalists in order to get varying perspectives. This aided his search of written sources. His review of the topic area thus contained both written sources and original interviews, and so added extra authority to that part of his thesis.

However, you have to be selective and careful in your use of people. If you buttonhole someone for hours on end they will probably not be as helpful as they might be if you were to carefully sort out what you wish to discover and occupy as little of their time as possible.

Before considering people and networks as sources of topic information, there is an ethical aspect in seeking support and advice from others. In the set book by Cryer (2000) there is a short chapter (chapter 12) which is very worthwhile studying. It also considers your role in providing others with support and advice. Remember that you have a wealth of experience yourself, and getting together with other students and sharing your research experience can help you all. Even if your projects are very different, tips on doing research and getting around problems can be remarkably generic! For part-time students an e-mail network can be a useful way of keeping in touch, coupled with the occasional meal or drink at a mutually convenient location.

ACTIVITY 5.4

Read chapter 12 of Cryer (2000), pp. 140–5, on co-operating with other researchers and complete her activities.

Methods of contacting people

There are many ways of identifying 'people in the know' in your field. The following are just a few.

1   *Conferences*. An obvious place to find key people in your subject area. A good way to get going, as you do not have to contact anyone out of the blue. Start talking over coffee or lunch.
2   *Arrange an interview*. (Offer to buy a drink or, if very important, lunch.) Also telephone interviews are increasingly acceptable, particularly for busy people.
3   *Organise a workshop* on your subject. This may sound daunting, but how about a research students' workshop initially? Your supervisor may be able to help set one up. If you are an external student, your internal supervisor should know of other research students in your field of study.
4   *Give a seminar*. This may sound ambitious, but it can be very useful even if it is about discussing how you plan to do your research. You can see several people at once rather than running around to see them. You may even end up with a 'steering group' to draw upon for advice.
5   *Set up a computer conference*. A good idea if there are very few people in your subject area. It could then lead on to a face-to-face meeting.

FIGURE 5.1
A first-year
PhD student
presentation
on project
method and
research
plans

6   *The Internet* is a useful way to identify people. You could set up a home
      page on your project. People in the know might then start contacting you.

To find people you will often need to trace the organisations for which they
work. Techniques to do this should be in an information search guide to your
subject area. Information on the organisations themselves is often useful and
may help you to select whom you approach. Make sure you check the organisation section in any information search guide you use.
      Key people include:

1   *Other researchers* – this is obvious.
2   *Authors*.
3   *Journalists*, who are a wonderful source of 'who is doing what'. Their time
      is often limited, so restrict yourself to a quick call unless you have a really
      good introduction from someone who knows them.
4   Many 'serious' documentary programmes have an Internet site (and in
      some cases scripts are available on request).
5   *'Stakeholders'* in the subject area, in other words, people who are responsi-
      ble for part of what you are studying. They should know what research and
      developments are under way on their patch. Such 'stakeholders' are not
      just sources of data once your research is under way; they can help you
      design and develop your research project itself. Who knows, your contacts
      may pave the way to a job!

'People' sources are often the best ways to find out about the so-called 'grey literature', such as company reports, unpublished research documents and conference

proceedings. These often do not get on to databases (although some now cover these sources). In fast-moving and emerging topic areas the less formal types of literature are often very important.

But remember that you must prepare yourself to talk to people. Unfocused and lengthy discussions do nothing but annoy. This does not mean that you cannot contact people from the beginning of your research, but you must be clear about the basis on which you are contacting them. For example, it is perfectly acceptable to talk to even a leading expert in your field about whether the preliminary ideas for your project make sense and whether they know of anyone else doing something similar.

Keeping it organised

As noted at the beginning of this chapter, you will end up using information on other people's research for different purposes throughout your own project and when writing up the results. Keeping records of what you have read and found, and of who you have contacted, is thus very important. If you do not have good records, you will end up having to do more or less the same work all over again!

Therefore it is important to make notes and classify literature and other information obtained according to what it contributes to your project. Clearly, this is a function for your research journal, but you will need to have a system to record and keep track of information you have obtained. Information search guides usually provide advice on recording your search (electronic or on paper), and it is as well to heed their advice.

ACTIVITY 5.5

Read chapter 8 of Cryer (2000), 'Keeping records', particularly the section on 'Keeping records of what you read' (pp. 101-3). Complete the activity on pp. 102-3. Cryer's main point is that, however you record your literature and contacts, with literature you must keep complete references for when you write them up in your dissertation or thesis (p. 70, 'Documentation of literature').

Finally, as this chapter has emphasised, you will be using information on other people's research in your subject area throughout your own research. Make sure you keep in touch with the body of research and researchers. Write up as you go along; talk to people; share your discoveries, frustrations and joys. You are now not just studying a topic – you are *part* of the 'topic'!

Reference

Bruce, C. S. (1994) 'Research students' early experiences of the dissertation literature review', *Studies in Higher Education*, 19 (2), pp. 217–29.

Appendix 5.1   Reviewing the literature

Any investigation, whatever the scale, will involve reading what other people have written about your area of interest, gathering information to support or refute your arguments and writing about your findings. In a small-scale project, you will not be expected to produce a definitive account of the state of research in your selected topic area, but you will need to provide evidence that you have read a certain amount of relevant literature and that you have some awareness of the current state of knowledge on the subject.

Ideally, the bulk of your reading should come early in the investigation, though in practice a number of activities are generally in progress at the same time and reading may even spill over into the data-collecting stage of your study. You need to take care that reading does not take up more time than can be allowed, but it is rarely possible to obtain copies of all books and articles at exactly the time you need them, so there is inevitably some overlap.

Analytical and theoretical frameworks

Reading as much as time permits about you topic may give you ideas about approach and methods which had not occurred to you and may also give you ideas about how you might classify and present your own data. It may help you to devise a theoretical or analytical framework as a basis for the analysis and interpretation of data. It is not enough merely to collect facts and to describe what is. All researchers collect many facts, but then must organize and classify them into a coherent pattern. Verma and Beard (1981) suggest that researchers need to

> identify and explain relevant relationships between the facts. In other words, the researchers must produce a concept or build a theoretical structure that can explain facts and the relationships between them ... The importance of theory is to help the investigator summarize previous information and guide his future course of action. Sometimes the formulation of a theory may indicate missing ideas or links and the kinds of additional data required. Thus, a theory is an essential tool of research in stimulating the advancement of knowledge still further.
>
> (Verma and Beard 1981: 10)

Sometimes 'model' is used instead of or interchangeably with 'theory'. Cohen and Manion explain that

> both may be seen as explanatory devices or schemes having a conceptual framework, though models are often characterized by the use of analogies to give a more graphic or visual representation of a particular phenomenon. Providing they are accurate and do not misrepresent the facts, models can be of great help in achieving clarity and focusing on key issues in the nature of phenomena.
>
> (Cohen and Manion 1989: 16)

The label is not important but the process of ordering and classifying data is.

As you read, get into the habit of examining how authors classify their findings, how they explore relationships between facts and how facts and relation-

1

ships are explained. Methods used by other researchers may be unsuitable for your purposes, but they may give you ideas about how you might categorize your own data, and ways in which you may be able to draw on the work of other researchers to support or refute your own arguments and conclusions.

The critical review of the literature

An extensive study of the literature will be required in most cases for a PhD and a critical review of what has been written on the topic produced in the final thesis. A project lasting two or three months will not require anything so ambitious. You may decide to omit an initial review altogether if your reading has not been sufficiently extensive to warrant its inclusion, but if you decide to produce a review, it is important to remember that only relevant works are mentioned and that the review is more than a list of 'what I have read'.

Writing literature reviews can be a demanding exercise. Haywood and Wragg comment wryly that critical reviews are more often than not uncritical reviews – what they describe as

> the furniture sale catalogue, in which everything merits a one-paragraph entry no matter how skilfully it has been conducted: Bloggs (1975) found this, Smith (1976) found that, Jones (1977) found the other, Bloggs, Smith and Jones (1978) found happiness in heaven.
>
> (Haywood and Wragg, 1982: 2)

They go on to say that a critical review should show 'that the writer has studied existing work in the field with insight' (p. 2). That is easier said than done, but the main point to bear in mind is that a review should provide the reader with a picture, albeit limited in a short project, of the state of knowledge and of major questions in the subject area being investigated.

Consider the following introduction to a study by Alan Woodley (1985) entitled *Taking Account of Mature Students*. You may not be familiar with their field of study, but does the introduction put you in the picture? Does it give you some idea of the work that has been done already and does it prepare you for what is to follow?

> Of the many who have looked at the relationship between age and performance in universities none has as yet produced a definite answer to the apparently simple question 'Do mature students do better or worse than younger students?'
>
> Harris (1940) in the United States found evidence to suggest that younger students tended to obtain better degree results.

Similar findings have been made in Britain by Malleson (1959), Howell (1962), Barnett and Lewis (1963), McCracken (1969) and Kapur (1972), in Australia by Flecker (1959) and Sanders (1961), in Canada by Fleming (1959) and in New Zealand by Small (1966). However, most of these studies were based on samples of students who were generally aged between seventeen and twenty-one and the correlation techniques employed meant that the relationship between age and performance really only concerned this narrow age band. As such, the results probably suggest that bright children admitted early to higher education fare better than those whose entry is delayed while they gain the necessary qualifications.

2

This view is supported by Harris (1940) who discovered that the relationship between age and performance disappeared when he controlled for intelligence. Other studies have shown that those who gain the necessary qualifications and then delay entry for a year or two are more successful than those who enter directly from school (Thomas, Beeby and Oram 1939; Derbyshire Education Committee 1966).

Where studies have involved samples containing large numbers of older students the results have indicated that the relationship between age and performance is not a linear one. Philips and Cullen (1955), for instance, found that those aged twenty-four and over tended to do better than the eighteen and nineteen-year-old age group. Sanders (1961) showed that the university success rate fell until the age of twenty or twenty-one, then from about twenty-two onwards the success rate began to rise again. The problem with these two studies is that many of the older students were returning servicemen. They were often 'normal' entrants whose entry to university had been delayed by war and many had undergone some training in science or mathematics while in the armed forces. Also, while Eaton (1980) cites nine American studies which confirm the academic superiority of veterans, there is some contradictory British evidence. Mountford (1957) found that ex-service students who entered Liverpool University between 1947 and 1949 were most likely to have to spend an extra year or more on their courses and more likely to fail to complete their course.

Some studies have shown that whether mature students fare better or worse than younger students depends upon the subject being studied. Sanders (1963) has indicated that the maturity associated with increasing age and experience seems to be a positive predictor of success for some arts and social science courses. The general finding that older students do better in arts and social science and worse in science and maths is supported by Barnett, Holder and Lewis (1968), Fagin (1971), Sharon (1971) and Flecker (1959).

Walker's (1975) study of mature students at Warwick University represents the best British attempt to unravel the relationship between age and performance. He took 240 mature undergraduates who were admitted to the university between 1965 and 1971 and compared their progress with that of all undergraduates. This gave him a reasonably large sample to work with and the timing meant that the results were not distorted by any 'returning servicemen factor'. His methodology showed certain other refinements. First, he excluded overseas students. Such students tend to be older than average and also to fare worse academically (Woodley 1979), thus influencing any age/performance relationship. Secondly, he used two measures of performance; the proportion leaving without obtaining a degree and the degree results of those taking final examinations. Finally he weighted the degree class obtained according to its rarity value in each faculty.

The following findings achieved statistical significance:

(i)   In total, mature students obtained better degrees than non-mature students.
(ii) In the arts faculty mature students obtained better degrees than non-mature students.
(iii) Mature students who did not satisfy the general entrance requirement obtained better degrees than all other students.

3

(iv) The degree results of mature students aged twenty-six to thirty were better than those of all other mature students.

Several other differences were noted but they did not achieve statistical significance due to the small numbers involved. The mature student sample only contained thirty-three women, twenty-six science students and thirty-seven aged over thirty. The aim of the present study was to extend Walker's work to all British universities so that these and other relationships could be tested out on a much larger sample of mature students.

(Woodley 1985: 152–4)

This review is more thorough than would normally be required for small projects, but the approach is much the same, whatever the exercise. Alan Woodley selects from the extensive amount of literature relating to mature students. He groups certain categories and comments on features which are of particular interest. He compares results of different investigators and discusses in some detail a study by Walker (1975) which serves as a pilot for his more extensive study of mature students in British universities.

The reader is then in the picture and has some understanding of what work has been done already in this field. Woodley no doubt omitted many publications that had been consulted during the course of his research. It is always hard to leave out publications that may have taken you many hours or even weeks to read, but the selection has to be made. That is the discipline which has to be mastered. Once you have identified possible categories from your initial reading, and have your cards in order, you will be able to group the source material, and writing the review becomes much easier.

Note

The references in this offprint are not listed as this is not necessary for its use in this book.

Acknowledgement

From J. Bell, *Doing your Research Project: a guide for first-time researchers in education and social science*, second edition (1993), Buckingham, Open University Press, chapter 4, pp. 33–8.

4

Chapter 6

Using Computers in Research

Martin Le Voi

After reading this chapter you will:

- Realise the variety of uses to which IT can be put

- Know where to start exploring various aspect of IT

- Develop good habits when using software, for example using style sheets in word-processing, taking breaks from the computer

- Have an idea of the resources available to you

Ways to use information technology

No academic discipline has been left untouched by the information technology (IT) revolution. Whether it is CD-ROM collections of historical texts, sophisticated algebra processors or computer-based control of laboratory equipment, computers have found a role to play everywhere. It is hard to imagine doing a research project nowadays without them. There are many ways in which IT can assist researchers and we will be covering them in this chapter.

This chapter describes the main uses to which computers can be put in research. Computers are perhaps best thought of as information processors. The kind of information they process can be organised as words, graphics, numbers, ideas, records or messages. We shall look at each of these kinds of process to see how they can help with research. It is important to emphasise that this section will not attempt to teach you how to use each of these types of package, because there are plenty of tutorial guides, including purpose-written student guides, to enable you to learn specific items of software. One major aim of this chapter is to develop your awareness so that you and your supervisor can identify training material and/or training courses in various packages you need.

Commercial software for computers has targeted several routine jobs, which is of great help to researchers. These jobs are:

1   Writing a thesis with a word-processor.
2   Managing a bibliography.
3   Handling simple numerical operations.
4   Creating presentation graphs.

Computers are also used for:

1   Project management.
2   Communications (e.g. electronic mail, conferencing and file transfer).
3   Information search and retrieval (e.g. Web browsing, bibliographic searches).
4   Specialist software (e.g. statistical analysis, modelling).

Writing a thesis with a word processor

Word processors have transformed writing a thesis, which of course lies at the heart of doing a research degree. Page layout and editorial corrections are easily handled, and most word processors include spelling correction and grammar-checking facilities. Almost any modern word processor will make writing a thesis a good deal more manageable.

Although computers help greatly in writing a thesis, many academics still prefer to write early drafts with pen and paper, because ideas can be set down rapidly and moved around easily. Writing can of course also be done when a computer is not available. It can be hard writing straight on to a word processor on a computer screen, especially since scanning backwards and forwards to find things you wrote previously may be problematic. If, when you start writing, you tend to stare into space a lot, considering what to write next, you may find sitting in front of a computer screen rather uncomfortable. It is important not to spend too long at a time sitting at a computer. (There are more details about the correct way to use computers healthily and safely in Chapter 7; see also Chapter 4, 'The writing process'.)

Outlining a document

Modern word processors have innovations which are particularly helpful when writing large documents. Many have an 'outline' facility (sometimes also known as 'ideas processors') which allows you to construct the outline of a large document by creating a series of headings and subheadings in a hierarchy of levels. The content of each section you create is then attached to the subheading under which it appears. The benefit comes later when you decide that perhaps subheading 1.2.3 would be better under section 2.1. In outline, you can pick up that section, drop it into the new position and watch as all the sections are automatically renumbered in the new order. Changing the organisation of your work becomes easy to do and straightforward to manage. This can be very useful, especially as supervisors or examiners are notorious for asking that sections be moved around from one chapter to another. A computer also keeps track of footnotes, placing them correctly and renumbering them if they are moved.

Style sheets

One of the most useful aspects of modern word processors is the facility to build in standard text formatting as you write, using style sheets, templates or other forms of coding. This facility is frequently misused or ignored by new authors, and emphasises the need for getting appropriate training on the word processor you are using. Style sheets allow you to identify common elements in your thesis, such as chapter headings, headings, subheadings, quotations and figure captions, and to bring them all together under correctly identified styles. For example, the heading of this section is 'Heading 2' in my style sheet. Equally this text is 'Normal' in my style sheet, which defines the typeface, size of type, and even that there is an automatic gap between paragraphs. The pay-off is that it allows you to alter the layout of your document from beginning to end by changing a common style, which the computer then applies to all parts of the document with that style code. Thus all headings could be changed to a different font or style of emphasis by a single command. Using an enforced style also ensures a consistent layout, and the user does not have to try to remember on each occasion how to set out, say, indented quotations or figure captions. It is a common mistake for authors to forget to use style sheets and it is a mistake they invariably come to regret as they wade through hundreds of pages, changing layout commands one by one. So do make sure you learn to use your word processor correctly and try to get the appropriate training for writing a substantial document with a consistent layout.

Bibliographical software

One particular innovation in word processors, or at least in the 'add-ons' you can get for using with them, is a bibliographic package. Your written thesis is sure to include hundreds of references to existing academic work and to have a list of such references at the end. By systematically collecting your academic references in a bibliographic package, you can automate both the correct presentation of references in your text and the creation of the reference list in your chosen format. A good bibliographic package can change the format of this reference list depending on the required format of the academic publication to which you want to submit papers (see Figure 6.1). It is therefore an extremely useful package for people writing academic papers: see the discussion in Chapter 5, 'Undertaking a topic review'.

In this book we emphasise from the outset the importance of writing, so make it a priority to become familiar with the word processor you want to use right from the start, getting training if necessary.

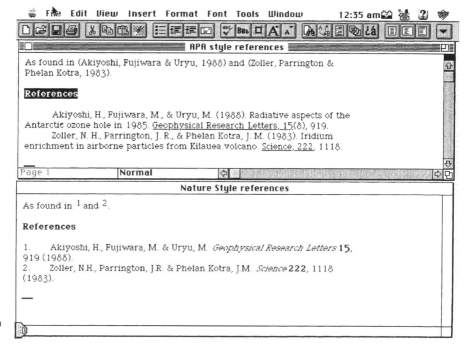

FIGURE 6.1
Screen shot of Endnote in action. The two documents are identical except for the selection of style

---

ACTIVITY 6.1

Consider the benefits a word processor will bring to you in writing up your thesis. Have you ever written such a large document before? Would you benefit from using an outlining function to allow you to 'play' with the structure of your thesis? Will you want to reuse the material for publication, and therefore benefit even more from style sheets and bibliographic packages, which make it so easy to change the appearance to suit the 'market'?

Spreadsheets (number processors)

In the numerical domain, the equivalent of a word processor is a spreadsheet. This allows you to manipulate numbers, or anything that can be quantified, in a systematic way using formulas and calculations. Modern spreadsheets are highly sophisticated and can handle things like days of the week, dates in general and other data which are more loosely translated to quantitative form. If your research is data-intensive, spreadsheets can provide a very useful preprocessor of data, allowing you to filter and sort data so that you can select different subsets for use in more sophisticated analytical programs. Indeed, many statistical packages now include spreadsheets as part of their data input technology. If your research is not data-intensive, spreadsheets can still be useful for all kinds of quick analyses which may be important to your project. You should be familiar with their capabilities so that you can quickly use one to do any analysis you need to. They are particularly suited to creating graphs of data of all kinds – whether pie charts, time series or histograms of categorical information – which brings us to the general area of creative graphics on computers.

Presentation graphics and drawing

You could perhaps call drawing packages 'picture processors'. Drawing programs are very useful for creating the diagrams and illustrations you need to include in your thesis. Again, it is important to try to understand fully the capabilities of your drawing programs so that you can use them appropriately. Of course, drawing packages do not substitute for the skill required to create good drawings, so it is often the case here that 'garbage in' produces 'garbage out'! However, with some practice you will be able to produce quite passable diagrams for use in your thesis.

A slightly more recent innovation in graphics processors is a package for producing presentation materials. These are essentially computer packages aimed at helping anyone giving a face-to-face presentation (that is, lectures or conference presentations) to create highly professional visual aids which allow them to put messages across to the audience in the most effective way possible. These presentation aids look most slick when running directly from a computer on to a large screen. Special-purpose projection techniques allow dynamic presentations of visual material, including text, diagrams, photos and also video clips, all of which can be controlled easily by the presenter, who does not have to leap around swapping slides on an overhead projector. If your presentation cannot make use of a computer to control the displays, presentation graphics packages allow you to create high-quality slides for use with conventional overhead projectors, with the careful use of colour, and appropriate use of textual layout (including a suitable choice of fonts and font sizes). Graphs and charts from spreadsheets can also be copied on to slides and pictures.

ACTIVITY 6.2

If you have given presentations in front of an audience before, consider how your talk could be improved with just a few visual aids. Or if you have written essays or research reports, think about how illustrations (whether graphs, charts or abstract diagrams) could have helped clarify your points. I have done this for this chapter!

Databases

Databases can be characterised as *record processors*. They are designed for a user who has large collections of records, all of which contain common information. The information can be categorical, numerical, verbal or nowadays even pictorial. By keeping large numbers of records in a common format, the advantage of databases is that they allow summaries of these records in ways which are very helpful to the user. Thus records can be sorted, counted and selected into subsets according to multiple logical operations.

If you follow the advice above and decide to equip yourself with a bibliographic package, you will launch yourself into using a database. Academic references contain all kinds of common information, such as journal titles, year of publication and authors. By keeping them in a convenient database, all these records can be accessed and manipulated in sophisticated and very useful ways. Again, time spent early on in mastering the functions of a database will save much frustration later on, so make sure you get to know the full capability of any database you decide to use in your research.

Figure 6.2 shows data entered into a bibliographic package. Two records and the corresponding sections of the database are shown. The information about journal title, volume number, page range, etc., is kept as 'plain' text and numbers. Only when a reference list is compiled do you ask for specific text formatting, such as italics and bold, as shown in Figure 6.1. The package then

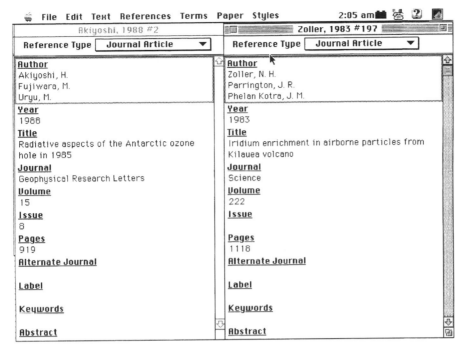

FIGURE 6.2
Raw data for biblio-graphical entries in Endnote

applies the requested formatting to the whole references section – a procedure notoriously prone to error if attempted by hand, one reference at a time.

Box 6.1 shows the information held in another reference database – PsycLIT – which holds references for articles in psychology, including an English abstract as well as other information, especially manually identified 'key words'. These allow key word searches, a very powerful information search technique (see pp. 147–8).

BOX 6.1

Record 1 of 6177: PsycLIT Journal Articles 1991–9/97

TI: Model of the function of the neostriatum and its neuronal activity during behavior in monkeys.
AU: Tolkunov, -B.-F.; Orlov,-A.-A.; Afanas'ev,-S.-V.
IN: Russian Academy of Sciences, I. M. Sechenov Inst of Evolutionary Physiology & Biochemistry, Lab of Integral Brain Functions, Moscow, Russia
JN: Neuroscience-and-Behavioral-Physiology; 1997 Jan-Feb Vol 27(1) 68–74
IS: 00970549
LA: English

PY: 1997
AB: Studied the properties of neostriatum neurons ... (PsycLIT Database
Copyright © 1997 American Psychological Association, all rights reserved)
KP: computer model of neural network and parallel recording of spike activity
of neostriatum neurons during performance of sequential actions; monkey;
translated article
DE: CAUDATE-NUCLEUS; ELECTRICAL-ACTIVITY; NEURAL-NETWORKS;
„NEURONS-; PUTAMEN-; MONKEYS-
CC: 41460; 41
PO: Animal
UD: 9709
AN: 84–33861
JC: 1550

Record 2 of 6177 – PsycLIT Journal Articles 1991–9/97

TI: The parallel transfer of task knowledge using dynamic learning rates based
on a measure of relatedness.
AU: Silver, –Daniel–L.; Mercer, –Robert–E.
IN: U Western Ontario, Dept of Computer Science, London, ON, Canada
JN: Connection-Science-Journal-of-Neural-Computing, – Artificial-Intelligence-
and-Cognitive-Research; 1996 Jun Vol 8 (2) 277–294
IS: 09540091
LA: English
PY: 1996
AB: With a distinction made between two forms of task knowledge transfer...
(PsycLIT Database Copyright © 1997 American Psychological Association, all
rights reserved)
KP: multiple task learning method of parallel domain knowledge transfer;
learning rate and task relatedness
DE: NEURAL-NETWORKS; TRANSFER-LEARNING
CC: 4160; 41
PO: Human
UD: 9709
AN: 84–33860
JC: 3549

Integrated packages

Integrated packages are simply collections of three or four different computer
programs which allow a user to do several functions in an integrated way. In
other words, you will see word processors integrated with spreadsheets and
drawing packages and databases. The result is that documents can be written

which include word-processed information along with tables and graphs created direct from spreadsheets and reports created direct from databases. Whenever the records change in the database, the word-processed document automatically alters to keep track of those changes. This level of integration is often very useful, particularly if you are expecting to include substantial data elements in your documents. However, many modern computer systems automatically allow the integration of data between programs that run on them by means of mechanisms built into the computer itself, without requiring you to buy complete packages from one manufacturer.

Project management

Doing a research degree is a substantial enterprise, requiring you to go through several stages of work, such as literature searching, data collection, data analysis and report writing, in order to produce your final written thesis. Often you will have to not only manage your own time but also co-ordinate your research with the availability of other sources of information, whether it is access to historical documents in far-flung libraries, access to sophisticated laboratory equipment available only in certain locations (such as astronomical telescopes), or access to other people for use as subjects of study themselves (for example, interviewing or experimental procedures). Scheduling and integrating all these processes appropriately into the progress of your research is effectively using skills to do with project management.

As noted in Chapter 3, in a research project, various activities rely on the completion of previous stages in the process, and frequently several different activities occur concurrently. In the early stages of your research, for example, as well as receiving training in the methodologies you are likely to use later on, you may also be doing a literature search while simultaneously contacting organisations you want to research or arranging visits to use laboratory equipment. Project management techniques are essentially formalisations of ways to manage these conflicting demands systematically and efficiently, which can be very useful in helping you to plan and manage your time as a research student. (Figure 6.3 shows an example.) Once again, it is important to understand the essentials of project management and the package you are using in order to benefit best from it.

ACTIVITY 6.3

Project management is discussed in Chapter 3, 'Planning and organising a research project'. Are there aspects of the scheduling of your research which concern you? Check with your supervisor how best to ensure that you can keep everything on track.

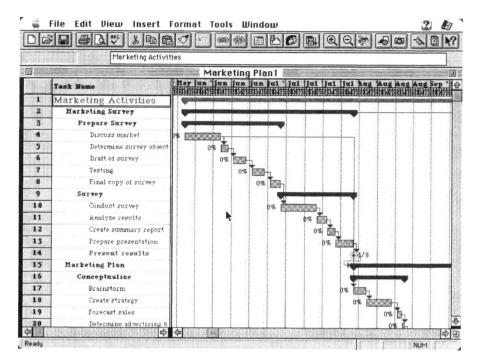

FIGURE 6.3
Screen shot
from
Microsoft
Project

Communications

Computers are making major changes in how we communicate between ourselves. Electronic communication in the academic environment is very well
advanced through the efforts of national networking bodies and the development
of the Internet. The increasing sophistication of the transmission of digital information down analogue telephone wires has meant that computers around the
world, and of course their users, can be in direct touch with each other.

Electronic mail and directory services

Electronic mail (e-mail) is in principle perhaps the simplest form of electronic
communication, in which electronic messages, usually but not exclusively simply text, are sent from person to person via their computers. E-mail allows messages to be sent to anyone in the world rapidly and with a high degree of
reliability. Nowadays, as well as text-based information, documents, graphics,
sound and even video can be transmitted. The advantage of e-mail over, say, fax
transmission is that the message can be dispatched to your own mail server without you having to make contact with the receiving server at exactly the time you
send the message. Your server arranges for your message to be delivered whenever the recipient can accept the mail, and any bottlenecks in transmitting the
message over the international links are avoided.

Like any communication system, if you want to send a message to someone, you need to know their address. Electronic addresses are in general never completely obvious even if the mailboxes try to use a person's real name (and in some messaging systems this is far from the case). An important element of e-mail support therefore is in directory services, which provide ways of looking up e-mail addresses. These are nowhere near as ubiquitous as they need to be to be useful, and it is still often difficult to find someone's electronic mail address if they have not given it to you personally. Nevertheless, there are some electronic directory services, such as X.500, which can help you find the addresses of other e-mail users.

Conferencing

E-mail allows you to send a message on any topic to anyone you wish, whether to just one person or to a list of people you have compiled. Conferencing extends this idea into creating an environment in which group discussions can be held; a single topic of interest is considered and discussed by several contributors who all submit their thoughts in electronic form for everyone to read (see Figure 6.4). The idea is to replace medium-sized face-to-face meetings discussing individual topics, sometimes because it is largely impracticable to assemble everyone who should take part in the same place at the same time. The discussion can be either moderated or unmoderated. In an unmoderated conference there is a free-for-all – all contributors are free to make any comment they want, however unrelated it may be to the stated topic of the conference. In a moderated conference, one or more people monitor incoming contributions to ensure that they are relevant to the topic and that they adhere to common standards of decency and/or legality.

Electronic conferencing can be a valuable medium for peer group discussion when problems of space or time prevent face-to-face meetings. However, the dangers of digressing from the topic domains are ever present and frequently lead to some people withdrawing from the topic, or even from the conferencing system.

The simplest form of electronic conferencing software is simply a large mailing list set up so that anyone on the list can send a message to anyone else. There are thousands, if not millions, of different *list servers* set up in this way to allow people to communicate about all kinds of subjects in which they have a common interest. These can be on any topic, and include discussions on technical and academic subjects. They are particularly useful when a subject is so

---

ACTIVITY 6.4

E-mail and conferencing are notorious for eating up time. Who are the people with whom it is most valuable for you to get in contact? Is there a discussion group dedicated to the topic of your PhD? (See pp. 147–8 for help.)

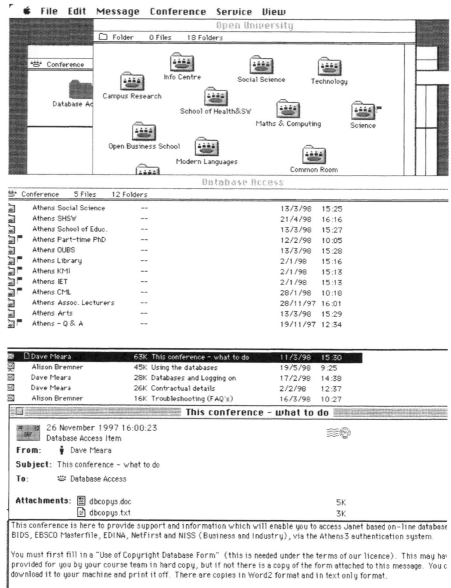

FIGURE 6.4
Screen shot
of FirstClass
conferencing
system

highly specialised that the number of people doing research in the area is very small (perhaps twenty or fewer) and may be widely scattered around the world. Related to these list servers are so-called *news groups*.

File transfer

File transfer between computers, otherwise known as *document transmission*, can occur in two ways. The author of a document can decide to send the document to someone else by e-mail if the mail system supports the transfer (which most modern e-mail systems do). Alternatively the author of the document can leave a copy in a publicly accessible area on a computer, to which anyone can connect and obtain a copy. The latter is a very common way of creating repositories of academic papers in machine-readable form, so that anyone can obtain a copy. The application used to access the data is sometimes called FTP (file transfer protocols). There are various programs on different computers which allow you to connect to public areas on servers and 'download' a file from them (including Web browsers: see the section on the World Wide Web below).

Dial-in remote access by modem

Increasingly, networks are accessed from home using a computer and a *modem*. The modem connection cannot provide the speed of access available to people using direct connections on a university campus, being ten to a thousand times slower. However, the convenience of being able to do some work from home and the fact that many simple operations, particularly e-mail, require the transmission of only small amounts of data mean that it is an increasingly popular method of communication. Anyone who uses a modem for such connections will know that you are at the mercy of the often surprisingly variable quality of a telephone line connection to your house. The result can be rather mysterious things occurring with the connections, and a certain degree of frustration. These problems are decreasing, however, and dial-in access is becoming a perfectly reasonable connection method. It is very important when you consider buying a modem, or gaining access via an internet service provider (ISP), to ensure that the modem you use on your computer will work satisfactorily with the destination modems provided by the ISP.

Because (in the United Kingdom, at least) a dial-in line costs money for every second connected, e-mail and conferencing systems often support *off-line readers*. With these, when you dial in to your communication system, the computer grabs as much relevant information (for example, e-mail messages) as fast as it can and then immediately disconnects, allowing you to read your communications at leisure without running up your telephone bill. However, a number of ISPs now provide unlimited internet access (either off-peak or at all times) for a fixed monthly fee, and so there is less need for off-line reading.

The World Wide Web

Earlier it was mentioned that communication has been transformed by the United States' development of the Internet. The Internet is basically a catastrophe-resilient network of electronic communications. 'Catastrophe resilient' means that, in the event of a large-scale war, many sections of the network could be destroyed but the rest would carry on undamaged. This is of importance since the Internet can carry military traffic. The Internet is essentially a *carrier* of electronic information around the world. What distinguishes the more recent incarnation of the Internet as the 'World Wide Web' is the form in which that information is stored globally and the mechanisms for accessing it.

'Surfing the net' using a 'Web browser'

World Wide Web information is held in the form of *hypertext* documents which are transmitted to your computer using hypertext transmission protocol (http). A hypertext document is one which does not simply present information on a screen but has so-called *hotspots* (or hyperlinks) which the user can click on with a pointing device. These hotspots lead to a reaction from the computer which is sensitive to the context where the hotspot is found. The action that occurs as a result of selecting a hotspot is manifold; it could be presenting a new page of text, showing a video, playing a sound or initiating a search for information. While this sounds complicated, in fact the behaviour of the computer should be predictable from the context in which the hotspot is found. As a result, the user should not be confused by what happens. Recent extensions of the definition of a hypertext document mean that selecting a hotspot can result in new software programs being transmitted to the computer, which can then perform highly sophisticated functions akin to that of a complete computer program such as a word-processing or spreadsheet package.

Searching for useful information: using search engines

There has been an explosion in the amount of information accessible on the World Wide Web this way. So much information is now available that it is impossible to search for it manually and hence there are various computer-based *search engines* which allow fairly sophisticated electronic searches of the entire global Web. The increasing sophistication of the search engines, and the increasing ubiquity of information providers on the Web, mean that as an information resource it is rapidly becoming an indispensable tool for all kinds of activities including, in your case, academic ones (see Figure 6.5 for an example). The kind of information sources you can expect to find are:

1   Pages provided by professional organisations (e.g. the AUT).
2   Information about forthcoming conferences.
3   Special interest groups in highly specialised academic pursuits.
4   Information about the academic staff in various university departments, including their research interests and publications.
5   Direct and easy access to publications held in central electronic collections.
6   Bibliographical information and access to electronic journals.
7   Library collections and facilities.

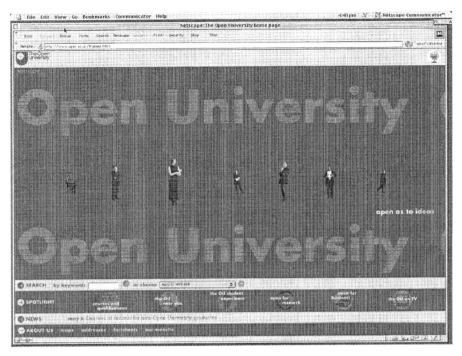

FIGURE 6.5
OU home
page on the
World Wide
Web

ACTIVITY 6.5

If you are unfamiliar with what is available on the Internet, ask your supervisor or your department's IT facilitator to book you on to an introductory course. Part-time students could visit an Internet (or 'cyber') café to check it out: these are springing up around the country, and many public libraries have Internet-connected computers. Also, most quality newspapers have a 'net' supplement one day a week which is worth a look. The Open University has a specific distance taught course to train and build confidence in using the Internet. This is entitled T171, 'You, your computer and the Net', and is available to anyone in the United Kingdom or other EU states.

The Cryer (2000) set book also discusses use of the World Wide Web (pp. 251–6).

Information search

Searching for information is one of the most important ways of making the best use of the Internet. There are several search engines which concentrate on different aspects of searching the Web, and which produce different kinds of summaries of information. Therefore it can be important to use the correct search engine, depending on what you are looking for.

Another important area of information search is in using the specifically academic sources of information that are available, such as BIDS (Bath Information and Data Services). Such resources are based in libraries.

Library indexes and other library resources are increasingly being made available through the World Wide Web. These areas will allow you to find the extent of resources available to you in the library itself, and indeed access a substantial number directly (including an increasing number of electronic copies of paper-based journals). See also Chapter 5.

ACTIVITY 6.6

This activity should take about an hour.
From any 'connected' computer, run a Web browser and connect to the on-line net skills interactive course at http://www.netskills.ac.uk/TONIC/ (see Figure 6.6). Use this course to familiarise yourself with World Wide Web concepts and activities.

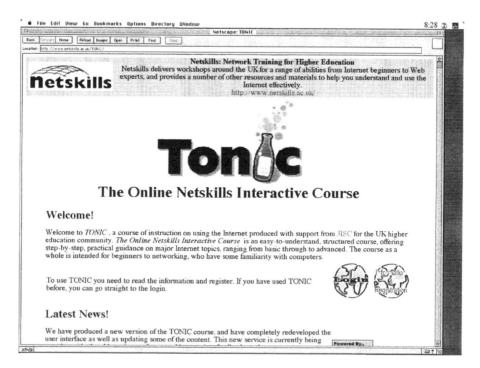

FIGURE 6.6
Tonic home page

Specialist analytical software and databases

For your research you will probably need to use computer software that is specific to your research programme and related disciplines. There are various areas in which sophisticated computer programs may assist you and your supervisor should advise you of what is available. Specific examples are given in Appendix 6.1.

Qualitative analysis packages

Just because data do not fit easily into a numerical measurement scheme, it does not mean that they cannot be analysed in a systematic way. Indeed, the less structured the form of the data, the greater the sophistication of the analysis required. When the data are completely unstructured, there is little alternative

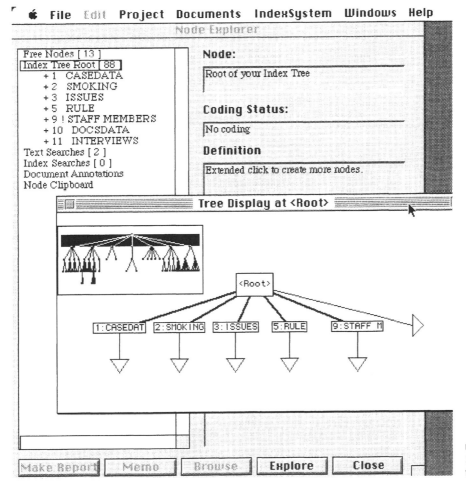

FIGURE 6.7
Screen shot from Nud-ist

but to rely on the most sophisticated analytical device around, namely the professional human researcher! However, before that point is reached, there are some highly sophisticated qualitative data analysis packages that may be of use to you. (Figure 6.7 shows an example.)

Quantitative analysis packages

Most quantitative analysis packages come in the form of statistics packages. Modern statistics packages have an enormous range of available statistics and in terms of functionality there is frequently very little to choose between them (see Figure 6.8). You should make sure you are familiar with your chosen package and can use it to do the analyses you want to do.

Modelling

Modern sophisticated mathematical and algebraic modelling packages can take much of the chore out of constructing models. Modelling is itself a varied problem, so it is important to choose the package that will be best suited to the kind of models you need to develop (see Figure 6.9).

Subject-specific databases

Nowadays many subject-specific databases are available on CD-ROMs, often in university libraries. There are also Internet-based databases to support research (see Figure 6.2).

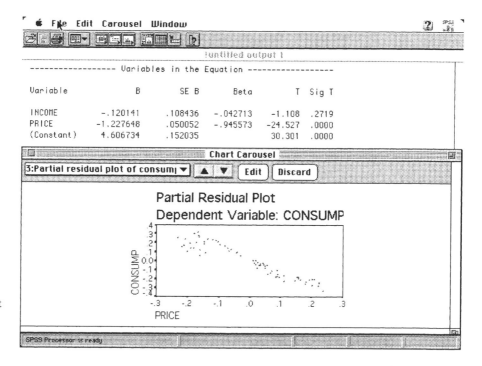

FIGURE 6.8
Screen shot from SPSS statistics package

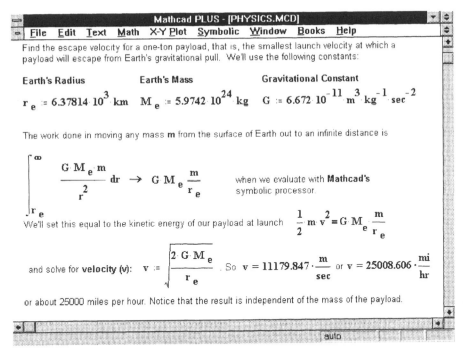

FIGURE 6.9
Screen shot from MathCAD modelling package

Conclusion

While computers can be an enormous help, they can also be addictive and eat up much valuable time. Remember to take care not to fritter away hours in unproductive work or Web searches. It is all too easily done!

Appendix 6.1 Open University recommended packages

The following advice is given to OU research students. Although the advice is appropriate to research students in any university, it is likely that if you are a full-time student at another institution your own computing department will have its own supported packages. Please check first to find out whether this is the case.

Core applications (word processors, etc.). Microsoft Word (for word processing), Microsoft Excel (a spreadsheet package), Microsoft PowerPoint (for presentation graphics), Microsoft Access (a database) and Hot Metal Pro (Web authoring) are recommended. Endnote is recommended as a bibliographical package.

Communications. AACS TST have various packages for mail, file transfer and remote access by modem. FirstClass software is widely used for conferencing and mail.

The World Wide Web. Netscape (a Web browser) is widely used. Among search engines are AltaVista, WebCrawler, Lycos, Yahoo.

Specialist analytical software and databases. NUD-IST (a qualitative data analysis package), SAS, SPSS and Statistica (quantitative analysis packages for statistics), Reduce (for mathematical and algebraic modelling) are used. The Open University Library (and all university libraries) has several CD-ROMs with subject-specific databases on them.

Acknowledgements

Grateful acknowledgement is made to the following for permission to reproduce the illustrations. *Figures* 6.1–2 © 1988–98 Niles Software Inc. All rights reserved worldwide. *Figure 6.3* copyright © 1990–95 Microsoft Corporation. *Figure 6.4* copyright © 1990–97 SoftArc Inc. *Figure 6.6* © 1997 Netskills, University of Newcastle. *Figure 6.7*, Qualitative Solutions and Research Pty Ltd. *Figure 6.8* copyright © 1994 by SPSS Inc. *Figure 6.9* copyright © 1998 MathSoft Inc. All rights reserved.

Chapter 7

Responsibilities, Rights and Ethics

Martin Le Voi

After reading this chapter, you will:

- Understand some of the responsibilities involved in academic research

- Understand the impact of the Data Protection Act on computer records

- Have an appreciation of Health and Safety considerations

- Understand basic copyright issues

- Be aware of ethical issues in research

Academic research is a major undertaking and needs to be taken very seriously. This is even more important when the product of the research is going to be a public document, such as a report or a thesis which will be available to the public in a library. Your work will be exposed to public scrutiny and, as a result, may be examined to see whether it is 'legal, decent, honest and truthful', in the words of the Advertising Standards Authority. Moreover, the process of doing your research must take due consideration of the moral, ethical and legal standards in research, as society currently sets them, and you must not take unacceptable risks with health (either physical or mental) – your own or anyone else's.

This chapter briefly considers the important aspects of responsibilities, rights and ethics for the researcher. The early sections apply to nearly all researchers, whereas later ones get more specialised, as they deal with issues such as animal and human experimentation.

Responsibilities

Academic integrity

Accuracy and honesty

Academic research is about creating a community of scholars which is sustained by both trust and scepticism. In theory, any piece of research by any professional academic should be capable of being repeated in order to test the reliability of the results. This is one reason why a research thesis has to take painstaking care to describe the research methodology used, so that it may be repeated by anyone wishing to do so. Academic research proceeds by new academics treating the work of previous researchers with due scepticism, usually questioning the interpretation and theoretical constructions arrived at in previous work.

In principle, previous research can be replicated in order to test whether the findings were reliable or just due to a lucky chance. While this can and does happen, by and large the community of scholars relies upon trust that other professional academics have done their research competently, effectively and, most important of all, honestly. For academic research to progress, this trust in the integrity of researchers is vital. If professional researchers started faking their results and making up the research they were doing out of thin air, research progress would quickly come to a standstill as it would rapidly become apparent that no results were trustworthy and that effectively there was no community of scholars operating.

You must therefore treat your research project with the utmost care. Do not succumb to the temptation to cheat and generate research results that you have not done, or pretend that you have found something which is not there. Not only does it jeopardise the whole conception of a research community of scholars, but also it will probably do you no good, as cheating is frequently found out. There are several famous cases where well known research published by leading authorities turned out to be at least suspect, if not actually fraudulent. Highly publicised allegations were made against Professor Cyril Burt for faking results in investigations of intelligence among identical twins in order to support his theories of intelligence. Although many of these allegations proved to be false, it remains highly likely that Cyril Burt at least probably generated some extra cases of identical twins (which are a rare occurrence among human births) in order to boost the size of his studies.

There are a few other cases of scientific fraud, which are usually very notable because of the huge publicity they generate. Fortunately, they appear to be rare. Scepticism of other researchers' work is usually aimed not at the raw data or original sources, but at their interpretation and the theoretical constructions from it. That is as it should be.

Plagiarism

While faking research is a case of fraud against the whole process of research, plagiarism can be described as fraudulently presenting ideas as your own when they are not. Perhaps it is more accurately described as theft, where someone else's ideas have been stolen and wrongly attributed. While this would not actually impede the progress of the research discipline, it is a serious breach of professional standards in research and one in which arguments can persist in long and bitter disputes.

It is important, therefore, that you carefully attribute all the ideas to which you refer in your work to their original authors, and any quotations you use should be accurate and appropriately referenced.

Confidentiality

Commercial confidentiality

Some research nowadays is carried out with the co-operation or the sponsorship of commercial organisations. When working with commercial organisations, you must take care not to breach any confidentiality that they expect to be maintained.

Some research studentships are funded by sponsorship from commercial or public bodies. Frequently, when these bodies commission research, they want to enter into an arrangement where they have control over the publication of the findings. This is not acceptable for research degree theses. A research degree thesis is *always* a public document, which will end up being available in the university library system for everyone to read. Sponsored research projects may occasionally result in theses which are not publicly available for a limited time, but after that time the documents will be made public. It is therefore particularly important in these cases that the thesis does not breach any other kinds of confidentiality about the research and the commercial environment in which the research was done.

Personal confidentiality and privacy

Since a thesis will be public, it is particularly important that the rights of sources are respected where necessary. Some of these issues are covered on pp. 160–63, so I will not dwell on them here. If you are obtaining information *about* individuals, it is clearly important that privacy is respected. If you are obtaining information *through* individuals (as informants), you may need to take steps to preserve their anonymity, as journalists try to do.

If you obtain private information, you must be sure to maintain confidentiality, both in your research thesis and with your research records. You may have to keep records under lock and key. Remember, there is a substantial understanding of trust between you and your sources, and ultimately your own academic integrity, perhaps also that of your profession, needs to sustain that trust and ensure that you conduct your research appropriately.

Using computers

Data privacy

It is worth emphasising that there is a strong moral duty to have due consideration for confidentiality and privacy in any subjects of research you may do. Only occasionally is that moral duty reinforced with legal protection. One such case is the Data Protection Act.

The Data Protection Acts

The Data Protection Act of 1984 relates to all automatically processed data on identifiable living individuals. Automatic processing generally refers to data held by a computer subject to computer processing. (This includes simple access and display, as well as more complicated data analysis techniques.) Data stored only on paper or in audio-visual recordings are not subject to the terms of the Data Protection Act, although they are subject to other ethical and legal considerations (for example, confidentiality and copyright issues).

If you are holding personal data which can be attributed to identifiable living people you will need to register that use. Your university will have a data protection co-ordinator who will supply the relevant forms and assist with registration.

Organisations (data users) are required to register all their uses of such data, and individuals (data subjects) have the right of access to data held about them (subject access). It is a criminal offence for a data user to operate outside the terms of its registered entry. Therefore it is essential that, before any new application is started, including, for example, the creation of any new database, your data protection co-ordinator is informed by completing a data protection questionnaire.

The 1998 Data Protection Act reinforces the terms of the 1984 Act, which it supplanted, as well as adding new measures. As well as automatically processed data on identifiable living individuals, manual (i.e. written) records are now included if they contain personal data, are stored in an identifiable filing system or are indented as a step in the procedure prior to automatic processing. The Act states that sensitive personal data must be processed 'fairly and lawfully'. When setting up any database it is therefore advisable to contact your data protection co-ordinator for guidance.

Health and safety

There are many aspects of health and safety. If you work in a laboratory you will receive detailed instruction in the health and safety aspects of working there. This may also apply if you are involved in fieldwork, depending on the hazards involved by the setting. Health and safety procedures are there not only to protect you but also to protect your co-workers or anyone else who may be adversely affected by risks associated with your research project. Similarly, others working in your field may impose risks on you and you need to be ready to respond appropriately to them.

It would be appropriate to look at your university's general health and safety guidelines. Guidelines on VDU and keyboard use are particularly relevant to all students. It is now known that excessive, unrelenting keyboard work can cause physical injury to the neural and muscular systems in hands and arms. Working in a comfortable environment and organising your work in a way that gives you adequate breaks from the keyboard are essential to your present and especially future physical health. Get into good habits now and you will not regret failing to do so later in life.

Rights

Intellectual property and copyright

Copyright is one of the areas of law falling under the broad heading 'intellectual property'. *Property* is a key term here. Like other forms of property in a Western capitalist society (such as land, buildings, manufactured goods and hand made artefacts), intellectual property can be owned, bought, sold, hired, inherited, etc. It is this ownership and those transactions that are governed by copyright law. Copyright is originated by an author. An author can keep or dispose of this property as he or she sees fit but, once it is passed on, it is gone to whoever has acquired ownership.

Much of the law is about definitions and protection of copyright from 'infringements'. Infringement of copyright could be considered a form of 'intellectual theft', and therefore there is a small industry involved in obtaining copyright 'clearance', which is basically permission from the copyright owner to use the intellectual property they own, usually for a fee. The owner often remains the owner in such cases. As important as copyright clearance are the allowable areas of use of intellectual property which do not infringe copyright protection as laid down in law. In these areas intellectual property may be used without requiring licensing from the owner. These important provisions are on pp. 159–60, covering exceptions to copyright protection, below.

What is copyright?

Broadly speaking, copyright is the protection given by law (as from 1 August 1989 in the Copyright, Designs and Patents Act 1988) to an author for his or her work. The word 'author' means not only writers but also artists (for example, painters, photographers and sculptors), composers, architects and people who write computer software. In addition, the Act gives protection to people who make sound recordings, cinematograph films, video recordings or cable programmes or who prepare editions of books, and to the BBC, the IBA and other broadcasters based in the United Kingdom for their broadcasts.

Generally speaking, copyright owners have the sole right to use their works or to authorise others to use them – although there are certain uses which do not constitute an infringement (see below for more details).

Because copyright is technically a form of property, it can be split up and transferred from person to person by gift, sale or licence or on death. So the author of a novel may grant and do separate deals with a US publisher for an American edition and with a French publisher for the French translation rights. At the same time, a film production company may have obtained an option to acquire 'theatric' rights in the novel (that is, the right to make a film for general release in cinemas: these rights generally include television rights in the material). As a result, finding the person who owns or controls the appropriate rights may sometimes be as time-consuming and difficult as negotiating the clearance that is required.

What copyright does not protect

There cannot be copyright in an idea or a suggestion as such (for example, the suggestion that the BBC should broadcast a *Mastermind* for teenagers), and accordingly the producer generally does not accept an obligation to pay for ideas, or to use one contributor's suggestion in preference to another. This does not mean that producers are always free to use the programme ideas submitted to them. In some circumstances, ideas presented to a producer may be protectable by an action for 'breach of confidence'. Moreover, if a suggestion takes the form of a detailed format for a programme, submitted in writing, the producer does recognise copyright in the format and, before televising programmes based on it, will arrange terms for its use with the author.

Who owns copyright?

The first owner of the copyright in a work is usually the person who brought the work in question into existence: for example, the author of a novel or article, the painter of a picture, the composer of a piece of music. In the case of films and sound recordings, the first copyright owner is the person who has made the arrangements to enable the recording or film to be made. Under UK law no formalities are required to vest the copyright in the original owner and, as explained above, owners may license various uses of the work and, indeed, may divest themselves of the copyright entirely by assignment. However, where a work is made by an employee in the course of employment, for example by a member of staff as part of their work, the copyright belongs to the employer. Where a member of staff creates something outside the course of their employment, the rights are their own. Contracts of employment may include clauses on copyright. For example, in the case of OU academic staff, the copyright in their teaching material belongs to the university, but with research materials copyright is the property of the individual.

For research students, who are not an employee, copyright in their work is their own. However, if a student's research is sponsored in any way, it is advisable to check whether there are any copyright or intellectual property rights clauses in the sponsoring agreement.

Exceptions to copyright protection

There are certain statutory exceptions to the general protection given to the owner of copyright.

Insubstantial part. A very short extract may be used without obtaining consent. The test of what constitutes an insubstantial part is as much a matter of quality as of quantity. It would be a substantial use of a copyright work to quote the line showing 'whodunit' in a detective story, and quotation from almost any copyright poem is likely to be substantial and therefore to require clearance; but the use of, say, 100 or 200 words from a full-length non-fiction book may be insubstantial.

Fair dealing. This is the more important exception and may allow relatively substantial use to be made of uncleared material in specific cases:

1 Research or private study.
2 Reporting current events (except in the case of photographs).
3 Criticism or review of the work itself or another work, provided you identify the work and the author. However, the use must be for a genuine critical purpose and not for biographical or general use. No hard-and-fast rule can be laid down about the length of the extract that can be used. It should be no longer than needed by the reviewer or critic for the purpose of making a point.

These 'fair dealing' exceptions apply under the 1988 Act not only to literary, dramatic, musical and artistic works but also to films, broadcasts or sound recordings. So the BBC can use a clip of a film or an extract from an ITV programme for review purposes or for reporting current events without obtaining consent, provided the 'dealing' is fair. In deciding whether any particular unauthorised use is fair or not, a court will probably attach importance to the impact, if any, that the unauthorised use has on the copyright owner's ability to exploit their copyright work commercially.

The 'fair dealing' exception is the one most commonly used in research theses. Provided the source of a work and its author are identified (hence the importance of a complete and accurate references section), academic sources can be quoted relatively freely. However, you may need to take care if your research involves gathering material to which copyright would apply (for example, oral history[1]), since you should address the issue of copyright when gathering the material if you want to use it freely.

Ethics

Ethical issues will most likely be highly specific to your particular research project. They will depend on whether you are experimenting on animals or humans, conducting interviews and surveys, using intrusive methods such as participant observation or action research, or doing scientific research with an obvious use as weaponry.

Interviews and surveys

When your research project involves interviewing, there are a series of issues that need consideration in advance. In particular, an interview is (usually) a one-to-one dialogue between two people, both of whom bring their own social background and personality to the situation. An interviewer must therefore decide on his or her intended relationship with the informants. Qualitative work necessarily entails involvement; it cannot be done in an 'objective', neutral, disengaged manner if it is to yield any worthwhile insight into the informant's world.

However, in most interview research the question of 'ownership' is quite clear: the research is planned and initiated by the researcher, and he or she 'owns the rights' to the data and the conclusions drawn from them. This makes for an uneasy relationship, and often a sense of guilt for the researcher, because he or she is not genuinely participating in the relationship, but rather using the informant as a source. There is no intention of continuing the relationship after the research is finished.

This may of course be a source of benefit to the participants under some circumstances; those who are in distress may sometimes welcome the chance to talk freely to a stranger and to work out their own attitude to what is happening to them without having to continue interacting with the person afterwards. However, there may be something distasteful to the researcher in using people for research purposes. It is particularly problematic where research is done in your own working environment or among friends or neighbours, because the degree of disclosure entailed by the research changes the nature of the relationships.

An alternative approach is full collaboration, where researcher and participant together set out both to solve a life problem and to write an account of the process. Some very successful research has been done in this way, mostly in the area of therapy (for example, co-counselling) or local 'political' change (for example, projects where groups of women have united to obtain some service from the local authority, or collaborative efforts to eliminate sexism or racism from school curricula). This kind of interview research does not lend itself to full collaboration. However, you may wish to introduce *some* element of collaboration into your research, some loosening of the power relationship between researcher and informants. It may be possible, for instance, to show your report to the informants and obtain their comments on it, or to run a group session to discuss your conclusions.

The important thing here, however, is not to promise what you cannot deliver. There should be some kind of 'contract' between researcher and informants – not necessarily a written document, but at least a series of implicit and/or explicit agreements by which the researcher is bound. You will need to promise your informants anonymity, for example – that what they say to you will not be used in a way which enables them to be identified – and you must keep that promise even if it is professionally inconvenient to do so. (Alternatively, if your research leads you to find things out about people over whom you have some control or power of decision, you must make your position clear to them.) If you have no power to remedy any 'wrongs' reported to you, that must also be made clear.

Any element of collaboration must be an explicit item of the contract, and you must make sure you will be able to deliver what you promise. Will there be *time* for collaboration, for example – will your report be written in time for a group meeting or for informants to read it? To what extent will such feedback interact with any promise of anonymity you wish to make? And what do you propose to *do* about the outcome of the feedback process? If the informants do not agree with what you have written, are you bound to change it? Or do you undertake to represent their views as well as your own, giving them the 'right of reply'? Or will you just take note of their reactions and use them if appropriate, retaining control in your own hands?

Human experimentation

Using humans as participants in experimentation is even more problematic than using animals. The well-being of the human participant must be paramount in considering the experiment proposed, and no experiment should be designed or intended to leave participants in a worse condition than when they began it, physically or mentally. In addition, experiments which deceive subjects or in other ways risk or intend to humiliate or otherwise morally compromise the participants may well be ethically unsound. One of the difficulties is that there is no clear dividing line over which one should not step, because of the inherent subjectivity of human experience. It is, in the end, a matter of professional judgement. Should you be contemplating such a research method, a useful set of guidelines is provided in the Ethical Principles of the British Psychological Society.

Animal experimentation

Animal experimentation raises important ethical considerations about the exploitation of animals for scientific work. The cost of using animals must be carefully considered and the experimentation must be legal, as well as ethical. This is such an important issue that most universities have specific guidelines for researchers that cover government legislation on the use of animals and agreed research practices. If your research is likely to involve any animal experimentation you must ensure that you are fully familiar with your own university's guidance.

Examples of ethically suspect studies

Any experimentation on animals involving pain needs the closest scrutiny. Early operant conditioning work in the 1950s used contingencies of negative reinforcement, which were designed to inflict pain on animals, as a means of shaping behaviour. These experiments were always controversial and remain so. Indirect distress to animals must also be examined: 'maternal deprivation' studies in the 1960s removed new-born primates from their mothers, with clear harmful consequences. Although the harm is indirect (and the procedure is almost routine in many farming practices), the utility of such experiments in science must always be evaluated.

In humans, the notorious experiments of Miller and Pribram, which deceived participants into believing they were administering harmful electric shocks to other humans, would be very contentious today. Even mild deception needs close scrutiny. Social experiments where participants (often unwitting) are deceived by role-playing collaborators (for example, staging robberies or heart attacks in the street) need close examination, even though such escapades are common in television scenarios such as *Candid Camera* or *Game for a Laugh*. It is important to note these media set-ups would be very unlikely to gain ethical approval in a scientific study, so the fact that a scenario has been tried on television is no defence. Many media outlets have no ethical monitoring procedure at all, beyond checking basic rights, such as privacy. For example, the vogue for real-life documentaries continues apace, although there is evidence that the intrusion of a camera crew is sometimes harmful to the participants. In a very early example, the BBC's *The Family*, the family portrayed subsequently broke up. Even though there had been a similar outcome for an American family in the same situation, the BBC was reluctant to concede the ethical point. Waivers signed by participants *never* absolve the professional researcher from considering their welfare.

Other social enquiries need careful thought. In an investigation of racial prejudice in public housing, is it justified to employ stooges of various races with fictitious backgrounds to tackle the administrative bodies under the pretence that they are in need of housing? Again, although many journalists would not hesitate, scientific investigators must apply the highest level of scrutiny to such proposals.

Incidentally, this is a real example of a study done at the Open University, which was criticised by the administering bodies for the deception involved. Whether those bodies would have been so critical had the study not unearthed substantial racial prejudice in their practices is a moot point.

Note

1   Copies of the Oral History Society's ethical guidelines are obtainable from the society at the National Sound Archive, British Library, 96 Euston Road, London NW1 2DB.

Acknowledgements

From C. D. Martin and D. H. Martin, 'Facing the computer ethics dilemma', in T. W. Bynum, W. Manner and J. L. Fodor, *Computing and Privacy* (1992), Research Center on Computing and Society.

Chapter 8

The Examination Process and the Viva

Stephen Potter

with contributions from John Swift

After reading this chapter, you will be able to:

- **Explore the purposes of a viva**

- **Understand how your examiners are appointed**

- **Understand what your examiners are required to do**

- **Prepare for your viva**

Why a viva?

Other chapters have covered how to prepare a written thesis. This one looks at the examination process and the oral examination – the viva voce (usually shortened to 'viva'). All research degrees in the United Kingdom entail a viva. For taught Master's dissertations a viva may be optional, depending on the individual course. In such cases the term 'presentation' can be used rather than 'viva', which is usually reserved for research degrees. A taught Master's presentation usually involves a student giving a talk on the dissertation, followed by questions from the examination panel. This chapter therefore refers only to research degrees, although several of the points raised could be useful for a presentation linked with a Master's dissertation.

Having written a thesis, you may well ask why you have to be put through the ritual of an oral examination. All research degree theses are subject to both internal and external examination; this ensures that they meet a general national standard. Why then do your examiners have to quiz you as well as evaluate your thesis? Indeed, there are moves in North America to phase out the viva for research degrees, the written thesis itself (marked by both internal and external examiners) being the sole basis of the award. To some extent, the viva is a tradition, but it does perform three crucial functions.

1   The viva is a check that the thesis is really the candidate's own work. Answering questions and discussing the content of a thesis show that you have not got another person to do the work for you or lifted large sections from somebody else's work. Such fraud is very rare, but not unknown.
2   As a PhD is intended to mark your emergence as a fully fledged researcher, the viva examines your ability to discuss and defend your research. This is part of being a researcher.
3   The third reason applies to every thesis and is a very important one. An examiner will have questions about how the research was designed, how it was undertaken, the conclusions drawn, or virtually any aspect of the work. A viva is where such matters can be raised, and it is the candidate's opportunity to further explain, justify and defend the way in which the research work was done.

There is a real danger that, if the award of a research degree depended only on marking a written text, an examiner might misunderstand what a candidate had done. The viva is a chance for the examiner to raise points of discussion and for the candidate to clarify the situation. If an examiner asked for modifications or a rewrite on the basis of the written text alone, the student could feel aggrieved if, in their view, such requirements were based on a misunderstanding or a genuine professional difference of opinion. In this respect the viva is to the candidate's advantage. In many ways not having a viva would represent a less fair examination process.

In addition, the viva gives you the opportunity to meet and debate with an expert from another institution. There is a good chance that the examiners will find your work intrinsically interesting. In some cases, ideas for publication and even further collaborative work and jobs have resulted from the viva.

The examination panel

Procedures for appointing an examination panel vary between universities, although they all follow a fairly similar pattern. It would be useful to check up on the procedures of your own university and/or discuss this process with your supervisor(s). This is something that should not be left to when you are about to submit your thesis, but should be clarified considerably earlier. This is because, although it is usual not to formally appoint examiners until shortly before a thesis is submitted, there is an informal process that leads up to this.

For example, at the Open University the formal process of setting up an examination panel is that, when a student gives notice of submission, the Research School asks the head of department to nominate a panel for the oral examination (viva). This is the formal procedure. In practice, your supervisor is the key person in approaching potential external and internal examiners. The head of discipline usually depends on a supervisor's advice to nominate the examiners. Although the practice of supervisors varies, once you are putting together the first draft of your thesis the question of who should be your external examiner should arise. Supervisors are expected to make informal approaches to potential examiners to check whether they are willing and available to examine a thesis.

The crucial choice is that of the external examiner, who really has the upper hand both in examining the thesis and in the viva. The extent to which your supervisor consults you about the choice of examiners is entirely up to them. A student cannot have the right to choose an examiner, but some discussion of the subject is acceptable and normal. However, it is crucial that the examination panel is entirely independent and unbiased. The OU guidelines state that examiners have to declare an interest if they are:

1   Planning to employ the candidate.
2   Planning to co-publish with the candidate.
3   A past student of the supervisor.
4   A 'regular' examiner for a particular supervisor or department.
5   Involved, or have been involved, with the candidate in a close personal relationship of any kind.

One additional point is that an examiner cannot be someone who has had a significant influence on the way you have designed and conducted your research, or who has collaborated closely with you. It is perfectly in order for your examiners to know you and be aware of your work, but they need essentially to be separate from your work in order to be able to examine it.

Your own university will have a set of rules governing the appointment of examiners. The rules usually require that examiners should be qualified in the subject area to be examined, should be members of the academic staff of a university or research institution, and normally should have experience in examining or supervising students.

It is normal for a UK examination panel to consist of one external and one internal examiner. However, particularly if the candidate's subject is multidisciplinary, or if an inexperienced examiner is involved, it is often possible to appoint a third examiner.

The role of supervisors can vary. In some universities a supervisor can be an examiner. In other universities this is not permitted, but in the latter case it is usual for one or more supervisors to attend the viva as an 'observer'. The supervisor/observer is not a member of the examination panel, but can be called upon by the examiners for advice and points of clarification.

ACTIVITY 8.1

What are you looking for in an examiner? Write down the sort of areas of expertise, abilities and characteristics that your examiner should have. The list could be helpful in discussing with your supervisor(s) the sort of person to be your examiner.

What happens in a viva?

The ordeal itself

There is no standard viva. A viva is usually completed in two or three hours. You, of course, should take a copy of your thesis to refer to (and do not forget a pen and paper, as you may need to take notes on a question). If you have any background material not in the thesis that might be useful in answering questions (for example, interview transcripts or experiment print-outs), it is perfectly acceptable to bring such material along.

One person will chair the viva. It is often the internal examiner, who is responsible for the examination being conducted according to your university's regulations and procedures, and is also responsible for completing the paperwork.

Examiners usually meet just before the viva to compare their preliminary impressions and to agree the main areas for discussion. A number of universities require the examiners to submit an initial report on the written thesis before they meet. These reports are compared and agreement is reached about who will ask what questions. Your supervisor/observer may also attend the meeting, although the regulations of some universities specifically forbid it.

Examiners may already have agreed informally on an initial recommendation and they can tell the candidate at the beginning of their viva. For example, a student could be told, 'We feel that the thesis is PhD standard, but we may require a few minor amendments to be made. We will discuss these with you.' However, don't *expect* this to happen.

Where appropriate, and with the agreement of both the candidate and the examiners, a viva can include the inspection of experimental apparatus, the demonstration of software, viewing of original data sources or any other reasonable request. For example, in one viva at which I was external examiner there was a request for the student to give a short verbal presentation on his thesis before we commenced questions. I agreed to this and found it very helpful in introducing me to the candidate and his work.

The examiners will, obviously, have read the thesis and will have prepared a set of questions to ask. These questions may be strategic (relating, for example, to the whole approach adopted or key ways in which the results have been interpreted) or tactical (for example, detailed aspects of the research method or points of clarification). You must be prepared for the fact that examiners largely ask questions about aspects they feel are unsatisfactory or unclear. If your work relates to a current controversy or debate in your subject area, the examiners are also likely to ask questions to make you address it. The upshot of such an approach is that you can get a rather negative impression of what is happening. The phrase 'defending a thesis' is often used, and perhaps it is not an inappropriate term. Many students feel they have been 'grilled', expecting the worst, only at the end to be congratulated on their work and told they have passed with no more than some minor corrections needed!

At the end of the viva the examiners have to complete a report recommending a result. For the Open University a form is used that specifically asks for comments on how the thesis displayed evidence of the competences required. (These were discussed in Chapter 2.) The examiners also have to comment on the candidate's 'defence of the thesis'. At universities that require an initial report before the viva, it is usual to ask the examiners to cover these points then, so the post-viva report is shorter.

The OU recommendation forms for a PhD, an MPhil and a BPhil are shown in Appendix 8.1. See if you can obtain a copy of the forms that your own examiners will use and look at the questions they are asked and the criteria set for them. They will probably be very similar to the OU forms.

When you are asked to leave the room at the end of your viva, most of the examiners' time is usually taken up sorting out what to write on the paperwork involved. You may be thinking that a great debate must be taking place as to whether your work is 'worthy' or not. In truth the examiners are probably trying to think up a suitable phrase to express how well you answered the questions they asked and whether 'good' is an acceptable comment for its presentation and style.

Possible results

It is worthwhile checking your own regulations, but in general, among UK universities, the following are the usual possible results from a viva.[1]

1   *The degree should be awarded.* In this case it is a simple matter of opening the bottles of fizz (or some other form of celebratory activity).

2   *The degree should be awarded subject to corrections and minor modifications.* In this case the correction of minor typographical errors or minor editorial amendments are deemed necessary. These need to be specified to the candidate, who will have a maximum time period in which to make them. The bottles of fizz are still very appropriate. This is the most common result of a viva.

3   *The degree should be awarded subject to substantial amendments (without re-examination).* In this case the thesis is considered to contain limited deficiencies that the examination panel is confident can be corrected satisfactorily by the student. Thus re-examination is not needed, but a time period is usually specified in which to make the substantial amendments. This result is still worth a bottle or two, but hold some back for after the amendments have been made.

4   *Major revision and resubmission with re-examination.* This result (sometimes called a 'referral') means that, in the examiners' view, the candidate's work is essentially on the right lines but needs some improvement before it can be finally accepted. The candidate is therefore given the opportunity to make major specified revisions and resubmit for examination and viva by the same panel. Again there is a time limit (typically up to two years) for resubmission. A referral is often viewed as rather traumatic, but in fact it is far from a disaster. However, it is probably best to keep the fizz in the cellar for the time being.

5   *Award as a lower degree than the one submitted.* In exceptional circumstances, many universities permit the examination panel to recommend that the thesis merits the award of a degree lower than that for which it was submitted. This may also be subject to minor modifications or amendments. It would be hard to recommend the fizz under these circumstances.

6   *Fail: no degree to be awarded.* This is an extremely rare recommendation. The examiners have to state as fully as possible why they were unable to make any other recommendation. If it happens, who cares? Open the fizz anyway.

Typically, about 20 per cent of research degrees are awarded with no changes needed; about 50 per cent are awarded subject to corrections and minor modifications; about 20 per cent are awarded subject to substantial amendment; 5 per cent require resubmission, and 5 per cent are awarded a lower degree than the one submitted. Remember that categories 1, 2 and 3 are all passes and that the most common recommendation is 2.

'When will I know the result?'

The examination panel usually informs the candidate of the recommendation either at the end of the viva or (as noted above) after the examiners have adjourned for a short discussion. If the candidate has to leave the premises, the procedure is to inform the internal supervisor, who lets the candidate know.

Preparing for your viva

Having described the sort of things that happen in a viva, how is it best to prepare? One important point is that several weeks will have elapsed between submitting your thesis and the viva. (In my case it was several months, but that is unusual today and most UK universities now specify that a viva should be within six weeks to two months of a thesis being submitted.) Consequently you will have probably been busy with other things and so you need to consciously get back 'up to speed' on your thesis.

The following is, perhaps, a typical experience:.

In my own case (OU full-time Systems PhD, 1990) I was busy with a new job during the weeks before my viva, so I didn't consciously prepare much, apart from rereading the thesis the day before. I did feel pretty well prepared, though: presenting conference papers and giving seminars over the years of the research; knowing a bit about my examiners (knowing two of them slightly myself and my supervisor knew the third one well); and being very familiar with my data.

On the day, the viva basically felt like a searching interview for a job which I felt I had a pretty good chance of getting. (Something which younger students may not have experienced, perhaps!) The chair set a constructive tone and everyone was friendly, if a bit formal. I was glad my supervisor was there, as he backed me up a couple of times, for instance by explaining that certain things in the rather lengthy thesis were included for the benefit of readers such as himself who were not very familiar with the field (e.g. the technicalities of NHS planning systems). At the end it was definitely a case of 'Open the fizz'; they didn't even want me to correct the typos!

Now that I am an examiner myself I value the memory of my own viva, and feel it should not be necessary to be hostile or confrontational. It should be a constructive event, particularly if the result is 'More work to be done'. One can still find out the candidate's weak points as a researcher without intimidating them as a human being! If they have the misfortune to be very arrogant, they may be inviting more difficult and relentless questions (I have seen this happen!), but

---

READING

There is a section in Pat Cryer's (2000) book on 'The examination' and on preparation for the viva (pp. 242–5 of the second edition). She also provides some practical hints on dress and conduct (pp. 245–6). It is worthwhile reading these two sections.

most candidates' behaviour will reflect nervousness rather than arrogance or over-confidence.

Strategies

Preparation for a viva can be seen in two ways, consisting of: (1) experience preparation, (2) specific preparation.

Experience preparation

Experience preparation alerts you to the type of experience you will have in the viva. One preparation method is to have a 'mock' viva. This is where the candidate has a dry run, with unfamiliar tutors acting as examiners, followed by feedback on the candidate's performance.

In a recent case, a student in the Open University's Institute of Educational Technology had a mock viva that simulated the real event as closely as possible. Two colleagues acted as internal and external examiners and were given the thesis to read four weeks before the 'viva'. The candidate said that one of the main advantages was that the mock viva made him think about his thesis from the point of view of other people, and it was especially useful for the parts he had taken for granted that people could understand.

The mock examiners asked the candidate for some items (records of research) that he had not thought of bringing to the viva. He consequently decided to do so, and it improved his confidence. Interestingly, the mock viva examiners came up with only one question that was asked by the real examiners. The specific questions asked will very much depend on the individual examiners.

It takes a lot of effort to set up a mock viva, and to be fully beneficial it must be taken seriously. It can provide an experience of a viva-like situation and give you an opportunity to discuss problematic areas and where you did not field questions well.

An easier alternative to a full mock viva is for your supervisor(s) to read your thesis and then ask you questions that they feel an examiner would ask. Again this provides experience in answering questions.

One danger of a mock viva is, if the actual viva ends up running in a totally different way, you could have had a misleading experience. As mentioned above, the questions will not be the same as in the mock viva (although one or two may be). As long as you are aware of how individual vivas can be, a mock viva can be helpful.

The sort of experiences provided in a mock viva can be obtained in other ways, which may be more practical for part-time students. They include:

1   A series of discussions between you and your supervisor(s) in the months leading up to the viva on what areas of the thesis you both think will attract the examiners' attention, what sort of questions they could ask and

how these might be answered. There could be a special tutorial on it a week or so before the viva.

2   Practise discussing your work and answering questions on it. For example, arrange seminars on your work in your final year, so as to build up experience in dealing with questions. However, do remember that questions in a viva are likely to be rather different. For example, in a seminar a speaker is unlikely to ask you what original contribution your research has made to a field of study.

Such activities can also help both you and your supervisor(s) to decide when you are ready to submit your thesis.

Specific preparation

Moving on to consider the specific content of your thesis, there are a number of methods to help you prepare for your viva.

1   Read through the thesis and make short notes of what is on every page or group of pages. For example:

> pp. 33–34, Craik and Lockhart model discussed.
> pp. 47–50, Wolfram's ontological theory debunked.

The result is a four- to six-page 'road map' of your thesis. This is valuable because:

(a) It gives point and focus to the rereading process, which makes it more effective.
(b) It makes sure you know what you have written.
(c) Commonly, in a viva, an examiner will ask a question which you are sure has been addressed in the thesis. It is perfectly possible that the examiner has missed a point or (even though they are not supposed to) has 'skim read' parts of the thesis. So instead of saying (unconvincingly) that you have covered the point somewhere and spending five minutes scrabbling through the pages (usually unsuccessfully), you can quickly scan down your notes and say, 'Ah yes, I debunked Wolfram on page 47.' This is enormously impressive to examiners (and could save you from being asked to do amendments of something you have already covered).

Phillips and Pugh suggest this technique and provide a more detailed guide on how to do it (pp. 153–5 of *How to Get a PhD*). An external PhD student of mine, to whom I gave a draft version of this text to help him prepare for his viva, said that he found making 'road map' notes particularly useful. At his viva he was asked more than once whether an issue had been covered. I was rather impressed by the way he glanced at his set of 'road map' notes and immediately turned to the page in his thesis where the point was covered. I think it impressed the external examiner as well!

2   Imagine yourself in the place of your examiner, having read your thesis and filling in something like the Open University's EX33 form recommending a result. Look at the form in Appendix 8.1 and consider:

     (a) What sort of questions would you ask to check out the criteria for your degree?

     (b) How would you try to create a constructive dialogue?

     (c) How would you try to put the candidate at ease?

     (d) How would you organise the order of points, of the questions and the discussion?

     (If you know anything about your examiners this can be useful. Certainly find out something about their own research, if possible.)

3   Ask the readers who are commenting on the thesis draft whether they have any examiner's questions they can give you.

4   Often, having submitted a thesis, a candidate reads it again and realises that, with the benefit of hindsight, its strengths and weaknesses are clearer. So reread your thesis carefully. If you think some parts might have been done better, be prepared to say that you now recognise as much and say how you would improve it. But also be ready to highlight what you know is really good. A common examiners' question is to ask in what way the work is original or has contributed to knowledge (which is one of the three criteria they have to report on). Be ready for it.

5   Be prepared to *enjoy* your viva. It is a wonderful opportunity to discuss your research with a group of people who actually want to know what you have to say. Relish it!

What may impress examiners

A good viva should be one where both the candidate and the examiners feel they have been enriched by the experience. So impressing the examiner is really a matter of getting this good, symbiotic relationship going. It can include:

1   Well considered replies that answer (and do not dodge or drift away from) the questions asked.

2   Flexible and agile thinking in response to unanticipated questions, backed up by argument and/or evidence.

3   Good understanding of appropriate research methods.

4   Critical awareness of the field of enquiry which demonstrates knowledge beyond that shown in the thesis alone.

5   Clear reasons for what is included and excluded from the research, and how this affects the results and conclusions drawn (e.g. 'to explore your question fully would have taken the research in a rather different direction, requiring a different methodology').

6   Self-critical assessment showing honesty in what has been achieved, partly achieved or not achieved at all.

7   Awareness of what remains to be researched and any key developments since the thesis was submitted (i.e. keeping up with the subject).
8   A sense of your personal desire to undertake the research, your search for answers, your integrity and your thoroughness.

ACTIVITY 8.2

1 Imagine yourself in the place of the examiner who, having read your thesis, is filling in the EX33 form recommending a result. (If you have obtained the documentation used by your own university, use that.) Look at the form and write down a list of questions that, were you your own examiner, you would need to ask about your thesis in order to fill in sections 5.2, 5.3 and 5.4.

Cryer (2000, p. 243, box 21.2) suggests three categories of questions to be prepared for, which relate to the 'form filling' questions:

(a) Research 'context': which debates, issues and problems your thesis addresses.
(b) The central idea that binds your research together.
(c) Your major contribution to knowledge.

Use these categories to begin to develop questions about your thesis.

2 Having written down these questions, think how you might answer them.

Helping your examiners

The anticipation and experience of a viva are almost certain to involve some degree of nervousness. A sympathetic panel of examiners will expect this. Remember that the purpose of the viva is to examine you at your best and not to create difficulties or inhibit your performance. It is therefore important to help your examiners. Also it is possible for the examiners to be nervous. The following points may help you to help them to help you!

1   Give straight answers to straight questions – resist the temptation to wander off the point (especially if you know you have a tendency to do so).
2   If you feel unsure whether you have answered a question fully or in the manner expected, ask the examiner if the answer is what they sought. This is not a sign of weakness but an indication that you want to offer a full and reasoned answer. Remember, the examiner does not know the thought processes you have gone through to arrive at your results or conclusions.

3   If you feel an examiner's question is unclear (as an examiner, I know I have asked some awfully vague questions!), always ask for clarification. The examiners will respect your need for accuracy – it reveals precision in your thinking.

4   Quite often what appears to be a single question actually contains two or more interdependent questions. Watch out for this. Point out that the question is of this nature, break it down and deal with the questions or issues in a stated order. Do not be worried about asking an examiner to remind you of the second or third part of their question.

5   If you think a question is based on a doubtful premise, challenge it (for example, if you think the examiner has missed the point).

6   When answering a complicated question, if possible state your answer simply and then elaborate further to support the answer.

7   In the face of a different explanation or interpretation from the one you have drawn, consider your response carefully. Examiners often do it to stimulate a discussion.

8   If it is an explanation you have considered and rejected, say so and why. If the examiner's explanation or perspective is new to you, think about its strengths and weaknesses and comment on them. For example, if you feel it misses the point of what your research explores, say so.

9   Examiners will not normally expect you just to accept their position. They welcome a discussion. Remember that an error of fact is unarguable, but an 'error' of explanation or interpretation is arguable.

10   If you make a mess of an answer, lose the point, or simply dry up, acknowledge it and start again. Everyone knows the occasion can be nerve-racking.

11   If you are surprised by a question, do not know the answer, or get flustered, do not be afraid to ask for time to think about it. For example, 'That's a good point which I hadn't considered. Can I think about it for a moment?' If you are still stuck, admit you do not have an answer. (You may be able to go back to it later.)

12   Things that give out the wrong signal to examiners are:

(a) False modesty.
(b) Exaggerated claims you cannot sustain.
(c) Distortion of facts to fit what you want.
(d) 'Flannel' to try to hide something.

13   Be friendly, honest, alert and interested and (difficult as it may seem) be yourself, not an image you have of the perfect candidate.

ACTIVITY 8.3

Having looked at the checklists above, are there any areas that you feel require particular attention? Discuss them with your supervisor(s).

After the viva

Chapter 22 of Pat Cryer's book is a brief consideration of life after the viva. For some reason she fails to mention the possibilities of food and drink, but she does offer the good advice that if any amendments are needed it is best to get them out of the way as soon as possible. Her careers advice may seem more appropriate to full-time research students; however, for many part-time students a research degree can be linked with career progression.

READING

Read this short chapter of Cryer (2000) now – or maybe read it after the viva when you are awaiting the result …

Appendix 8.1   EX33 research degree examination: examiner's joint recommendation and report forms

The first page of the Open University's EX33 form is the same for all research degrees, so only one example of it is included here. It is followed by the pages for the BPhil, MPhil and PhD versions of the form. The comments and names are fictitious, but are based on the author's experience of the sort of things examiners write about candidates' theses and their viva.

APPENDIX

EX33 RESEARCH DEGREE EXAMINATION – EXAMINER'S JOINT RECOMMENDATION AND REPORT FORMS

The first page of the EX33 form is the same for all research degrees, so only one example of it is included in this Appendix. This is followed by the pages for the PhD, MPhil and BPhil versions of the form. The comments and names are fictitious, but are based on the author's experience of the sort of things examiners write about candidates' theses and their viva.

THIS PAGE COMMON TO ALL RESEARCH DEGREES	SPECIMEN	**EX33 (PhD)** (August 2000)

Examination Panel Report Form

This form should be completed by the examination panel and returned by the internal examiner to the Research School on the day following the oral examination. At least one copy of the thesis must be returned with this form. Please indicate in Section 4 if a copy of the thesis is retained by the examiner(s) and/or candidate.

1.   Candidate Details

Candidate name: ...ROBIN COX...

Personal identifier: ..R0542850.......   Discipline: ...SOCIAL GEOGRAPHY........

Thesis title: ..EMISSION REDUCTION FROM CITY TRAFFIC : OPPORTUNITIES....
................AND SCOPE......

Degree for which submitted: **PhD**   Resubmission: Yes or (No)   Date of oral: ..25.6.98..........

> **FOR COMPLETION BY RESEARCH SCHOOL**
> Date of registration: ....   Date of submission: ....
> Scheme of study: Full-time   (Part-time external)   Part-time internal
> Highest qualification on entry: ....

2.   Examiner Details

Internal examiner/assessor : .........J.E. PRESTON...............

Post held   : ....PROFESSOR OF TRANSPORT STUDIES...............

External examiner   : ....K. HAMILTON...............

Post held   : ....READER URBAN STUDIES...............

External examiner   : ....

Post held   : ....

Observer at oral   : ....J. BROWNING...............

3.   Recommendation (see section 10.0 of the examination guidelines EX10)

We recommend: Tick one box

i)   the candidate be awarded the degree for which the thesis has been submitted   ☐

ii)   the candidate be awarded the degree for which the thesis has been submitted after satisfactory completion of corrections and minor modifications specified overleaf*   ☑

iii)   the candidate be awarded the degree for which the thesis has been submitted after satisfactory completion of substantial amendment specified overleaf but for which resubmission is not required*   ☐

iv)   the candidate be permitted to resubmit the thesis for re-examination for the degree for which it has been examined after major revision   ☐

v)   another recommendation as specified below (see 10.5 of the examination guidelines EX10)   ☐
....

vi)   that no degree is awarded   ☐

* Member(s) of the panel responsible for checking the changes to the thesis: ....
(See sections 10.2 and 10.3 of the examination guidelines.)

Open University form EX33: the PhD version, pp. 2–3

SPECIMEN

4.   **Copies of Thesis Returned**

Number of copies of thesis returned with this form: ....2..

Number of copies of thesis taken by student: ....1..

Number of copies of thesis retained by examiner(s) (please give details and reasons): ......1...........

..RETAINED IN ORDER TO COMPARE WITH CORRECTED VERSION....................

At least one copy of the thesis must be returned to the Research School after the examination.

5.   **Report on PhD Thesis**

The examination panel is asked to provide comments about how the thesis satisfies the criteria for the degree (see section 9.3 of the examination guidelines EX10).

(i)   Please comment on the presentation and style of the thesis.

GENERALLY WELL PRESENTED, BUT WITH SOME MINOR ERRORS
OF GRAMMAR.
FIG 4.2 UNCLEAR AND NEEDS TO BE REDRAWN

(ii)   In what way does the thesis show evidence of being a significant contribution to knowledge?

THE CANDIDATE PROVIDED NEW AND DETAILED INFORMATION
ON EMISSIONS AND REDUCTIONS FROM A RANGE OF POSSIBLE
PUBLIC TRANSPORT DEVELOPMENTS AND SHOWED CURRENT VIEWS
OF THE LINKS BETWEEN THE TWO ARE OVERSIMPLIFIED. FURTHERMORE
HE EXPLORED THE LIMITS OF EXISTING MODELLING TECHNIQUES,
INDICATING WHERE THEY ARE UNSUITED TO TAKING INTO ACCOUNT
KEY VARIABLES

(iii)   In what way does the thesis show evidence of the candidate's capacity to pursue further research without supervision?

THE RESEARCH INVOLVED SEVERAL STRANDS WHICH REQUIRED
CAREFUL CO-ORDINATION. THIS WAS SUCCESSFULLY ACHIEVED AND
INDICATES THAT THE CANDIDATE IS NOW A CAPABLE RESEARCHER.

SPECIMEN

(iv) **How much material worthy of publication does the thesis contain? Please indicate how much, if any, has already been published or accepted for publication.**

THE CANDIDATE HAS ALREADY PUBLISHED FOUR PAPERS BASED ON THE EARLIER PART OF HIS THESIS. TWO ARE IN REFEREED JOURNALS. WE DISCUSSED POSSIBLE PUBLICATIONS BASED UPON THE CONCLUDING CHAPTERS WHICH THE CANDIDATE WILL PURSUE.

6. **Please comment on the candidate's defence of the thesis at the oral examination.**

THE CANDIDATE WAS ARTICULATE AND RECEPTIVE TO THE CRITICISMS AND COMMENTS MADE BY THE EXAMINERS. HOWEVER SOME POINTS COULD HAVE BEEN DEVELOPED MORE VIGOUROUSLY.

7. **Please give any other comments on the thesis.**

In the case of recommendation 3(ii), 3(iii) or 3(iv) please provide detailed information about the corrections and minor modifications, substantial amendment or major revision that the candidate is required to undertake. Continue overleaf and/or attach an additional sheet as necessary.

CORRECTIONS AND MINOR MODIFICATIONS HAVE BEEN REQUESTED, WHICH ARE DETAILED IN A SEPARATE SHEET SUPPLIED TO THE CANDIDATE.

The Research Degrees Committee will formally ratify the recommended result on the basis of this report. Please ensure that detailed comments are provided in each relevant section, since a request from the Committee for clarification or elaboration will delay formal notification to the student of the ratified result. Please ensure that a copy of the thesis is returned with this form and that comprehensive details of any changes required by the examination panel are provided.

Signed : Internal examiner / assessor : ........J.C. Preston...

External examiner : ....K.Hamilton...

External examiner : ....

Date: ....25.6.98...

Open University form EX33: the MPhil version, pp. 2–3

SPECIMEN

4.   Copies of Thesis Returned

Number of copies of thesis returned with this form: ....4..

Number of copies of thesis taken by student: ....

Number of copies of thesis retained by examiner(s) (please give details and reasons): ....

....

At least one copy of the thesis must be returned to the Research School after the examination.

5.   Report on MPhil Thesis

The examination panel is asked to provide comments about how the thesis satisfies the criteria for the degree (see section 9.2 of the examination guidelines EX10).

(i)   Please comment on the presentation and style of the thesis.

THE THESIS WAS WELL WRITTEN AND EXCELLENTLY ILLUSTRATED. THE READER WAS GUIDED WELL THROUGH THE STUDENT'S RESEARCH, WITH EACH STAGE EXPLAINED CLEARLY.

(ii)   In what way does the thesis show evidence of candidate's proficiency in the methods and techniques of research?

THE CANDIDATE EXPLORED HOW PRODUCT BRANDING TOOLS AND PROCESSES THAT HAVE BEEN DEVELOPED FOR SALES IN SHOPS NEED TO BE ADAPTED FOR SELLING VIA THE INTERNET. SHE EXPLORED THIS ISSUE VIA A LITERATURE SEARCH AND THEN CONSIDERED THREE POSSIBLE RESEARCH METHODS BEFORE CHOOSING IN-DEPTH INTERVIEWS OF BRANDING MANAGERS IN STORES MOVING TO INTERNET SALES. THE METHODS AND TECHNIQUES WERE APPROPRIATE AND WELL CONDUCTED.

(iii) In what way does the thesis show evidence of an adequate knowledge and discussion of the literature in the specified field of study?

THE CANDIDATE CONDUCTED A THOROUGH LITERATURE SEARCH OF THE BRANDING LITERATURE, USING SPECIALIST DATABASES/CD ROMS AND ALSO CROSS-CHECKED THIS BY CONSULTING SPECIALISTS IN THE SUBJECT.

SPECIMEN

(iv) **Does the thesis demonstrate initiative, independence of thought and a distinct contribution to scholarship?**

THE CENTRAL QUESTION OF THE THESIS WAS ORIGINAL AND THIS ISSUE HAD NOT PREVIOUSLY BEEN STUDIED SYSTEMATICALLY OR FROM AN ACADEMIC PERSPECTIVE. IT IS A DISTINCT CONTRIBUTION TO SCHOLARSHIP

6. **Please comment on the candidate's defence of the thesis at the oral examination.**

THE CANDIDATE RESPONDED WELL TO THE QUESTIONS AND INITIATED A LIVELY DISCUSSION!

7. **Please give any other comments on the thesis.**

In the case of recommendation 3(ii), 3(iii) or 3(iv) please provide detailed information about the corrections and minor modifications, substantial amendment or major revision that the candidate is required to undertake. Continue overleaf and/or attach an additional sheet as necessary.

NO AMENDMENTS OR CORRECTIONS WERE REQUIRED. THIS WAS AN EXCELLENT PIECE OF WORK WHICH DESERVES AN UNQUALIFIED PASS.

The Research Degrees Committee will formally ratify the recommended result on the basis of this report. Please ensure that detailed comments are provided in each relevant section, since a request from the Committee for clarification or elaboration will delay formal notification to the student of the ratified result. Please ensure that a copy of the thesis is returned with this form and that comprehensive details of any changes required by the examination panel are provided.

Signed :   Internal examiner / assessor :   .....M.Y.Quin...

External examiner :   .....A. Ismail...

External examiner :   ....

Date: ....14.11.98...

Open University form EX33: the BPhil version, pp. 2–3

SPECIMEN

4.   Copies of Thesis Returned

Number of copies of thesis returned with this form: ....4..

Number of copies of thesis taken by student: ....

Number of copies of thesis retained by examiner(s) (please give details and reasons): ....

....

At least one copy of the thesis must be returned to the Research School after the examination.

5.   Report on BPhil Thesis

The examination panel is asked to provide comments about how the thesis satisfies the criteria for the degree (see section 9.1 of the examination guidelines EX10).

(i)   Please comment on the presentation and style of the thesis.

GENERALLY GOOD PRESENTATION

(ii)   In what way does the thesis show evidence of the candidate's ability to investigate critically a specific field of study?

THE CANDIDATE EXPLORED THE DEVELOPMENT OF GRAPHICAL USER INTERFACES (GUIs) AND PRESENTED A GOOD CASE THAT, ALTHOUGH COMPUTER GAMES ARE DEVELOPING POSSIBLY BETTER GUIs THAN USED (OR PLANNED) FOR OPERATING SYSTEMS, THERE IS SUCH A TECHNICAL LOCK-IN TO PRESENT GUIs THAT INCREMENTAL RATHER THAN RADICAL CHANGE IS MORE LIKELY.
THIS WORK DEMONSTRATES A CRITICAL INVESTIGATION OF THE SUBJECT.

(iii)   In what way does the thesis show evidence of an adequate knowledge and discussion of the literature in the specified field of study?

THE LITERATURE WAS WELL RESEARCHED AND USE WAS ALSO MADE OF WORKING DOCUMENTS AND COMPUTER ENGINEER PROJECT PROPOSALS THIS IS A SUBJECT THAT HAS A DIFFUSE LITERATURE - BUT THE CANDIDATE EXPLORED IT WELL

SPECIMEN

(iv) **Does the thesis demonstrate that the candidate has made a significant advance in her/his field beyond first-degree level?**

THE LEVEL OF ANALYSIS WAS CLEARLY BEYOND FIRST DEGREE LEVEL.

6. **Please comment on the candidate's defence of the thesis at the oral examination.**

THE CANDIDATE SOMETIMES HAD DIFFICULTY EXPRESSING THEIR IDEAS BUT WAS ABLE TO ANSWER ALL QUESTIONS TO THE EXAMINERS' SATISFACTION.

7. **Please give any other comments on the thesis.**

In the case of recommendation 3(ii), 3(iii) or 3(iv) please provide detailed information about the corrections and minor modifications, substantial amendment or major revision that the candidate is required to undertake. Continue overleaf and/or attach an additional sheet as necessary.

LIKE MANY BPHIL DEGREES, THE CANDIDATE HAD ACTUALLY DONE MORE THAN WAS NEEDED! HE CERTAINLY HAS THE POTENTIAL FOR AT LEAST A MASTERS IF DESIRED.

SOME MINOR CORRECTIONS WERE REQUIRED AND DETAILED TO THE CANDIDATE ON A SEPARATE SHEET

The Research Degrees Committee will formally ratify the recommended result on the basis of this report. Please ensure that detailed comments are provided in each relevant section, since a request from the Committee for clarification or elaboration will delay formal notification to the student of the ratified result. Please ensure that a copy of the thesis is returned with this form and that comprehensive details of any changes required by the examination panel are provided.

Signed :   Internal examiner / assessor :   M. Bletchley

External examiner :   W.S. GATES

External examiner :

Date: 1.12.97

Note

1   Again you should check your own university's regulations, as the wording differs and the time periods set for the submission of corrections will also vary.

Acknowledgement

Pages 171–76 of this chapter draws upon John Swift's 'The viva voce', in D Newbury (ed.) *The Research Training Initiative* VII (1997), Birmingham: University of Central England.

Index